Memoirs of the life of that learned antiquary, Elias Ashmole, Esq; drawn up by himself by way of diary. With an appendix of original letters. Publish'd by Charles Burman, Esq

Elias Ashmole

ECCO
PRINT EDITIONS

Memoirs of the life of that learned antiquary, Elias Ashmole, Esq; drawn up by himself by way of diary. With an appendix of original letters. Publish'd by Charles Burman, Esq

Ashmole, Elias

ESTCID: T066412

Reproduction from British Library

Half-title: 'Memoirs of the life of Elias Asmole, Esq;'. The half-title is unpriced; a variant has the half-title priced: "Price 1s. 6d". Pp. v-vii misnumbered vi-viii.

London : printed for J. Roberts, 1717.

viii[i.e.vii],[1],99,[1]p. ; 12°

Eighteenth Century
Collections Online
Print Editions

Gale ECCO Print Editions

Relive history with *Eighteenth Century Collections Online*, now available in print for the independent historian and collector. This series includes the most significant English-language and foreign-language works printed in Great Britain during the eighteenth century, and is organized in seven different subject areas including literature and language; medicine, science, and technology; and religion and philosophy. The collection also includes thousands of important works from the Americas.

The eighteenth century has been called "The Age of Enlightenment." It was a period of rapid advance in print culture and publishing, in world exploration, and in the rapid growth of science and technology – all of which had a profound impact on the political and cultural landscape. At the end of the century the American Revolution, French Revolution and Industrial Revolution, perhaps three of the most significant events in modern history, set in motion developments that eventually dominated world political, economic, and social life.

In a groundbreaking effort, Gale initiated a revolution of its own: digitization of epic proportions to preserve these invaluable works in the largest online archive of its kind. Contributions from major world libraries constitute over 175,000 original printed works. Scanned images of the actual pages, rather than transcriptions, recreate the works *as they first appeared.*

Now for the first time, these high-quality digital scans of original works are available via print-on-demand, making them readily accessible to libraries, students, independent scholars, and readers of all ages.

For our initial release we have created seven robust collections to form one the world's most comprehensive catalogs of 18th century works.

Initial Gale ECCO Print Editions collections include:

History and Geography
Rich in titles on English life and social history, this collection spans the world as it was known to eighteenth-century historians and explorers. Titles include a wealth of travel accounts and diaries, histories of nations from throughout the world, and maps and charts of a world that was still being discovered. Students of the War of American Independence will find fascinating accounts from the British side of conflict.

Social Science

Delve into what it was like to live during the eighteenth century by reading the first-hand accounts of everyday people, including city dwellers and farmers, businessmen and bankers, artisans and merchants, artists and their patrons, politicians and their constituents. Original texts make the American, French, and Industrial revolutions vividly contemporary.

Medicine, Science and Technology

Medical theory and practice of the 1700s developed rapidly, as is evidenced by the extensive collection, which includes descriptions of diseases, their conditions, and treatments. Books on science and technology, agriculture, military technology, natural philosophy, even cookbooks, are all contained here.

Literature and Language

Western literary study flows out of eighteenth-century works by Alexander Pope, Daniel Defoe, Henry Fielding, Frances Burney, Denis Diderot, Johann Gottfried Herder, Johann Wolfgang von Goethe, and others. Experience the birth of the modern novel, or compare the development of language using dictionaries and grammar discourses.

Religion and Philosophy

The Age of Enlightenment profoundly enriched religious and philosophical understanding and continues to influence present-day thinking. Works collected here include masterpieces by David Hume, Immanuel Kant, and Jean-Jacques Rousseau, as well as religious sermons and moral debates on the issues of the day, such as the slave trade. The Age of Reason saw conflict between Protestantism and Catholicism transformed into one between faith and logic -- a debate that continues in the twenty-first century.

Law and Reference

This collection reveals the history of English common law and Empire law in a vastly changing world of British expansion. Dominating the legal field is the *Commentaries of the Law of England* by Sir William Blackstone, which first appeared in 1765. Reference works such as almanacs and catalogues continue to educate us by revealing the day-to-day workings of society.

Fine Arts

The eighteenth-century fascination with Greek and Roman antiquity followed the systematic excavation of the ruins at Pompeii and Herculaneum in southern Italy; and after 1750 a neoclassical style dominated all artistic fields. The titles here trace developments in mostly English-language works on painting, sculpture, architecture, music, theater, and other disciplines. Instructional works on musical instruments, catalogs of art objects, comic operas, and more are also included.

The BiblioLife Network

This project was made possible in part by the BiblioLife Network (BLN), a project aimed at addressing some of the huge challenges facing book preservationists around the world. The BLN includes libraries, library networks, archives, subject matter experts, online communities and library service providers. We believe every book ever published should be available as a high-quality print reproduction; printed on-demand anywhere in the world. This insures the ongoing accessibility of the content and helps generate sustainable revenue for the libraries and organizations that work to preserve these important materials.

The following book is in the "public domain" and represents an authentic reproduction of the text as printed by the original publisher. While we have attempted to accurately maintain the integrity of the original work, there are sometimes problems with the original work or the micro-film from which the books were digitized. This can result in minor errors in reproduction. Possible imperfections include missing and blurred pages, poor pictures, markings and other reproduction issues beyond our control. Because this work is culturally important, we have made it available as part of our commitment to protecting, preserving, and promoting the world's literature.

GUIDE TO FOLD-OUTS MAPS and OVERSIZED IMAGES

The book you are reading was digitized from microfilm captured over the past thirty to forty years. Years after the creation of the original microfilm, the book was converted to digital files and made available in an online database.

In an online database, page images do not need to conform to the size restrictions found in a printed book. When converting these images back into a printed bound book, the page sizes are standardized in ways that maintain the detail of the original. For large images, such as fold-out maps, the original page image is split into two or more pages

Guidelines used to determine how to split the page image follows:

• Some images are split vertically; large images require vertical and horizontal splits.
• For horizontal splits, the content is split left to right.
• For vertical splits, the content is split from top to bottom.
• For both vertical and horizontal splits, the image is processed from top left to bottom right.

MEMOIRS
OF THE
LIFE
OF THAT
Learned *Antiquary*,

Elias Ashmole, *Esq;*

Drawn up by himself by way of Diary.

With an APPENDIX of original
LETTERS.

Publish'd by CHARLES BURMAN, Esq,

LONDON,

Printed for *J. Roberts,* near the Oxford *Arms,* in *Warwick-Lane,* 1717.

THE
PREFACE.

 HE bare Mention of the Person, whose Diary and Letters are now published, may sufficiently satisfie the World from whence they originally came, and where they are still preserved. The Copy, from whence these Papers are published, is in the Hand-Writing of ROBERT PLOT, LLD late Professor of Chymistry, Chief Keeper of the Ashmolean Museum in the University of Oxford, and Secretary of the Royal

Royal Society, and was by him transcribed for the *Use* of a near Relation
of Mr Ashmole's, a private Gentleman in Staffordshire, who has been pleased to think they may be acceptable to
the World for their Exactness and Sin-
gularity. They were collated a few Years
since by David Perry, M A of Je-
sus College in Oxford, and Head-
...person there of the Place, who correct-
ed from the original M. script (a)
some few literal Errors. The Chara-
cter of M Ashmole is so well known,
and so excellently, though concisely
drawn in these Papers, as well as in
that Article published under his Name,
in the Supplement to the learned Mr.
Collier's Historical Dictionary, partly
extracted from these Materials by
the justly celebrated Mr. Edward
Llwyd, Superior Bedel of Divinity
in the University of Oxford, that in
Recommendation of an obscure Editor
could do any Service, after so noted
Names

_____

(a) In... M S ... ... Num. 1135.

Names. The Usefulness of this Kind of Work, I shall not descant upon; but only say thus much, That they let us into the secret History of the Affairs of their several Times Discover the Springs of Motion, and display many valuable, though minute Circumstances overlooked, or unknown to our general Historians, and to conclude all, satiate our largest Curiosity

Newington
Feb 15-

CHARLES BURMAN.

THE

THE
LIFE
OF

Elias Ashmole, Esq.

In the Way of DIARY

Written by Himself.

I, Elias Ashmole, was the Son and only Child of Simon Ashmole of Litchfield, Sadler, eldest Son to Mr Thomas Ashmole of the said City, one of the chief Bailiffs of that Corporation, and of Anne, one of the Daughters of Mr Anthony Bowyer of the City of Coventry Draper, which his Wife only Daughter to Mr ... of Arley in the County of War-wick.

I was born the 23d of May 1617 (and as my dear and good Mother hath often told me) near half an Hour after 3 a Clock in the Morning

When I rectified my Nativity An 1647 I found it to be 3 Hours 25 Minutes 49 Seconds ☌ ♈ the Quarter 8 of ♊ ascending But upon Mr L ♈ rectification thereof Anno 1667, he makes the Quarter 25 ascending I was Baptized the 2d of Jun following at St. Mary's Church in L field My Godfathers were Mr Ch f, two of the Proctors of the Bishops Court and Mr   ffey, secrist of the Cathedral C

before I was carried to Church it was agreed my Name should be Th n (as was my Grandfather) But when the Minister had named the Child Con ner Offey answered F at which Pa ners wondered and being at their Return home asked, w f Reason she could render no Account but that it came suddenly into his M a more than ordinary impulse of S My Godmothers Name was Mrs Br g

When I was about a Year old and set by th ute I ht it, and burned the right si of my forehead it resting upon the Iron Ba s of wh I always re na near pre   fomething for
b

I as   h f w as also
S   n I was
b

young, b[ ] [k]now not the certain time of
[ ]ther

[ ]ing b[ ]t 8 or 10 Years old (but the
[ ] [ ]enr[ ]e remember, my Mother and I
[ ] [ ] o my Cozen B[ ] [ ] in L[ ]
[ ] time they wer[ ] building of a
[ ] [ ] [ ]ing up by Ladd[ ]s to the top
[ ] [ ]d down in which Fall th[ ] [ ]nfioe
[ ] [ ] [ ] struck again[ ]t th[ ] edge or
[ ] [ ] wh[ ]ch th[ ] [ ]r [ ] [ ]d a d[ ]p
[ ] C[ ] of which [ ] [ ]x a lo[ ]g
[ ] b[ ] [ ] scared

[ ] [ ] to [ ]t me Pu[ ] [ ]o [ ]
[ ] [ ] matri[ ]d on record Na[ ]
[ ] [ ] [ ] it [ ]s and V[ ]
[ ] a C[ ] C[ ]oner in L[ ]
[ ] [ ] a Suter who fir[ ]t was marri[ ]d
[ ] [ ] C[ ] [ ]hor of L[ ]ft[ ] [ ] and
[ ] [ ] D. [ ] n his Succeffor in th[ ] faid
[ ] [ ]lo[ ][ ]

T [ ] F. [ ] C[ ] [ ] [ ]the chief In
[ ] [ ] [ ] [ ] Pre[ ]e[ ]ts which I
[ ] [ ] [ ] C[ ] [ ]de t[ ] [ ]s M[ ] [ ]
[ ] h[ ] [ ] of [ ] [ ]nnt J [ ]n,
[ ] [ ] [ ] when [ ] w [ ] [ ]e,
[ ] [ ] [ ] [ ] [ ]me a[ ] Ac[ ] n
[ ] [ ] M [ ] [ ] [ ]
[ ] [ ] [ ] [ ] [ ] [ ]a[ ] to
[ ] [ ] [ ] [ ] [ ] [ ] [ ]me
[ ] [ ] [ ] to [ ] [ ] b[ ]
[ ] [ ] [ ] [ ]
[ ] [ ] [ ] [ ] [ ]t[ ]s at-
[ ] [ ] [ ] [ ] [ ] the[ ]-

in He was desirous I should spend part of
my Time in the Music School (having been
... ... at the Grammar School) and being competently Grounded therein I became
... ... in the Cathedral Church where
I remain'd being Baron for some up
to ...

... ... Mr T H...
...

... Organist of the Cathe-
... ... taught
... the Orga

... I ... of ... Organ my Journ-
... L... my Father and Mother
... me toward to the ... end of D Jo
Ha...

The ... of ... about ... a Clock before
Noon I entred L...

... this the before-mentioned Mr Twsan
died at the ... ... was buried the
... following in L... Cathedral in a
Chapel to the right Hand of the Lord S...
... Tomb, who was a Monument for D
... ... but ... down by the
Soldiers in the Parliament War

... ... a Physician in ...
... ... North east side...
... ...

... ... a
C... N...

... ... which gave
me Notice ... ... to ...
...

...

My Father was Born upon a *Whitsunday* in the Morning.

He was bred up by his Father to his Trade, yet when he came to Man's Estate, followed it but little. He more affected War, than his Profession and spent many of his Years abroad, which drew on him a Course of Expences and ill-Husbandry. His first Voyage was into *Ireland*, with *Robert* Earl of *Essex*, *Anno* 159 Two other Voyages he afterwards made, with his Son, *R* *t* *..* Earl of *Essex* into the Pala-nate from whom he received good Respect He was an honest fair Conditioned Man, *..d* *..d* *to* *others*, yet through ill Husbandry became *..* Enemy to himself and poor Fa-*..ar's*

.. *..* *..* year I was taught on *..* Harpsicher *..* Mr *...* who lay *..* *..* *..* *..* in *.. l* and *..* *.. ed h..* *..* *..* till *3..* *.. m* 1635-- *..* *..* *.. came to live at *.. ..* *..* *.. easant,* *.. .. ..* and lived *.. ..* the rest of *.. ..*

.. *..* *.. came to Snelland* to *M.. h.. .. ..* to ask his Content to marry *h.. ..* *.. ..*

.. *..* *.. .. and I went to *Snell-*

.. *..* *.. ..*

.. *..* *.. I am now Mr *Justice*

.. *..* *.. was Married to Mrs *k.. ..* *.. .. Daughter to Mr. *.. M.. ..*

B 3   B *..*

waring and Jane his Wife, of Smallwood in Com C st Gent She proved a vertuous good Wife The Marriage was in St Beneditts Church, near Pauls Wharf, by Mr. Adams, Parson there.

July 1 I and my Wife went towards her Fathers in Ch shire about Four post Merid where we arrived the 2ed of ...y

2c I took Possession of my House at Litch-
f d

Sept 1c My Uncle Thomas Ashmole, caused a Privy Sessions to be called at Litchfield, whereby I had some Trouble about my House there The Bill was found Ignoramus

Oct 5 I came to L c

In Mich Term I began to Sollicit in Chancery and had indifferent good Practice.

December 2c I went from London towards ch sh r

This Term I preferred a Bill in Chancery against my Uncle Thom Ashm

1629 Fe 5 I returned from Smallwood to L nd n

About the beginning of March Catherine Wife to my Brother Mr P t r Manwaring, and one of the Daughters and Coheirs of Mr New-
m of Poxr U in Com C st came to full age

M c first Mr a my Sister In Man-
w ne was brought to bed of her first Child

In Trinity Term (as I think) I became acquainted with Dr Thomas Caa man the Queens Physician About the beginning of July, Peter H ukh, Baron of Kind ren wrote to me to take

... upon me the Management of his Law
Business

... I went from *London* towards *Small-*
...

... I arrived at *Smallwood*

Octob. 12 I and my Wife returned towards
... beginning our Journey from *Smallwood*
this Day.

... I began to keep House, being
... at ... this Day

... 11 My Wifes Sister Mrs *Mary*
... full of an Ague, and having
had five Fits,

... She took her Bed

... *Past Mead* She dyed, and was buried in the Church of St *Clements Danes*, near
the Entrance into the Chancel She had a
very handsome Funeral, with Escotcheons of
her Arms in a Lozenge, pinned upon her Vel-
vet Pall

...9 M. Cousin *Philip Mainwaring* (a younger
Son of the House of *Keringham*) married *Mary*
the Daughter and Coheir of Sir *John Miller* of
...

... Mr *Dyer* Married Mrs *Miller*,
the other Coheir

... I took Lodgings in St *Clements*

... My Wife was brought to Bed of a
... Child, still born, about Noon, which
was buried the next Day

... I was Presented to the Lord Keeper
... and on the 12th Entertained by him

upon the Recommendation of my worthy Friend
Dr Cadirur

About the beginning of September, my Wife
fell Ill of a Fever

cast 31 I removed my self to a Chamber in the Midd'-Tmple in Em Cort, lent me by Mr Thomy Page

D r i Jor M g n my Maid, dyed of the Small Pox

 Ju 13 I began my Journey from S lix a to Lona

 I entred Lord r

F Mr Hll noved m t n Agreement th my Unc' The c h-

Fb I was admitted of C m s In

F 11 I was sworn an Attorney in the Court of Comn P as

Apr 22 William Care came to Lnd n to be my Servant he continued with me until 1615

21 He came to dwell ith e

May about the ginning of M my Maid Frakter C's fel sick of the Plague but escaped

3 I borrowed of my Cousin bam 70 l and paid t 20 June

Jun My Brother M received 2 from Mr Sm T upon a Mortgage of m La e

 I wa bound with my Brother for Pe f a of Cove about the beginning Towards the E Jn y Term I was sick for rt Dy

Aug

... I went to ...indsor. upon some Busi-
... for Dr Ca... being the first Time I
... this Castle.

... 2. I and my Wife went towards
...

... We came to ...

... Mr Wo... q...

... I went towards ... leaving my
... and ... h ca... b.g with Child

...

I came to lodge in my Chamber at C...

... My ... Wife fell suddenly sick
... and dicd to ... own Grief,
... of ... her ...end She was bu-
... Night about Nine of the Clock
... near the Entrance
... th ... of that Church, viz the
... that II

... I went from London towards

... A...ivi... at ...d I first heard of
... Death She was a virtuous m...
... ...ful, and ... Wife her Affection
... great ... me a... ...mu-
... h ... us to live to happily ...
... was ... beloved and esteemed
... Her ... Mother, insomuch as
... her Moth... be...ng near th...
... prof...d to the Baro... of
... ...fter told t...m; and
... knew ... whether she
... or ... on... ... better

18 I came to Smallw...

1642 Jan 15 I visited my dear Wifes Grave

Jan 18 I came from Smallw...d

2. I arrived at L...d...

F... Mr ... ... Pregit having proposed to me one o. hi Clerk Places in the ... Tr... ... Office the ... Day of D...mb.r last, but finding the Terms too hard I this Day resigned it t...

March 7 I removed my Goods to my Ch...

... Mr B... of ... nt -Inn and m... C... took a Journey first to see my old School M... Mr ... at Drayt... in Buckinghamshire then to ... fo into ...shr and thence to L...

20 The Trouble ... growing great, I resolved to leave ... C... and retire into the Country and this Day I... forward from ... to my Father-in-Law's House ...

... The ... Recor... of ... King ... I ... W... ...

... I ... with ... Cou...

12. I came first to Newcastle with the young baron of Kinderton

17 I returned into Cheshire with the Baron of Kinderton's Lady.

21 We came into Cheshire.

The rest of the Summer I spent at Kinderton, in assisting Mrs Venables, to get off the Barons Sequestration, but we could not prevail

Jul. 15 I went a second Journey into the North

21 I returned towards Cheshire.

5+6 The Beginning of this Year (as also part of the last) was spent at Oxford by Mr ... of Lichfield, and my self, in solliciting the Parliament there against Colonel Bagot, Governour of Lichfield, for opposing the Execution of the King's Commission of Excise (Mr ... and my self being Commissioners) whereupon by my Copy a Letter was sent to fetch the Colonel thither

... Mr P.. returned to Lichfield

... I first became acquainted with Certain Stars between Eight and Nine in ... Morning

... Certain Reasons moved me to be one of the Gentlemen of the Ordinance in ...

... was ... Second man of the Or-

... also entered a Souldier at my Bat-... Satisfaction

... rounded with my ...

I christened Mr For his Son at Oxford Mr dem

Mr Her on died my School Masters Wife

This Afternoon Sr John Heid n. Lieutenant of the Ordnance began to exercise my Gunners in Magd er Meadows

Mr Hurren was made a Captain of Horse

I saw Mrs M t in Braz-Nose Library being brought thither by Captain Swigfe p li Me This Day Mr M l mad a Motion to me to be a Commissioner of the Excise at Worcester

I was commanded to be Commissioner for the Excise at unknown to me which when I knew I accepted and prepared for my Journey thither

The King caused Mr _____ to be out of the Commission of Excise and mine to be inserted in his Place

Mr and my Son received the Commission of Excise from the Clerk of the Crown

Sir h h d gi e m a Letter of Recommendation to my Lord at of which this i Copy

MY LORD

T

are to be made known and serviceable to your Lordship, hath intreated my Mediation and Attestation, to whose Person, Industry, and Merits, during the Time he hath been interested in his Majesty's Service, under my Survey, I can no less than recommend him to your Lordship's Favour, as an able, diligent and faithful Man, wherein your Lordship may be ...... to believe,

Your Lordship,

Most Affectionate Servant,

JOHN HEYDON.

I took my Journey from Oxford to ...... Armed with Sir Charles Lu..... ...... and Merit. I arrived at .... Hor 15 Min and ...... Mr Jordan Mayor of Worcester, Mr ......, and my self, took the Oath as Commissioners of Excise in the Town-Hall and thence went unto the ...... and entered upon the Execution of the Commission. The Commission bears Test the ...... of December preceding,

...... I delivered Sir ...... Letter to my Lord Ashley who ...... me all Kindness, and to fix me in the Place of Artillery in the Garrison.

I ...... Mr Jordan the Mayor ...... Mr ...... Mr ...... Swing- ...... my self the Three Commissioners of ...... being met at W ...... Mr Gerard ...... have me Receiver and Register and

C   Mr

Mr ..... to be Comptroler, which was a-
greed un o

..... I first heard of my Mother Main-
.... Death from Mrs *Mary* ..... my
Lord .... D ughter

..... I received my
Con..... for a Cl..anship in the Lord
..... Regiment

Ap..... A new Commission for the Excise
came to .....

..... Colonel ..... Mr ..... and my
f .. took our Oaths to the said Commission,
..... Minutes .....

..... I was chose Register to the said Commission One H.. Minute .....

..... Mr ..... was sworn one of our Clerks
..... upon my Recommendation.
This Mr ..... was one of the Choir of *H*..
...., after the Surrender of the Garrison my
Servant some Year ..... upon the King's Return made one of the Ge..men of his Cha-
..el

..... walking in the
F.. a.. ..... where they were shooting
.. Ro.. an Arrow .... me but
I .... hurt Thanks ..... Go..

..... That ..... moved
..... Comma..... ..... ce ..
.. Fort .. .

..... Comma d ..
Com.....

..... O..... ..... I re
..... C ..... r C.....

July 1. Lichfield-Close was surrendered to the Parliament

July 1. Worcester was surrendered and the ... out of Town according to the ... and went to my Father Manwaring ...

... Mr. Richard Harrison Minister of ... and afterwards of L ...
... Mother Death and that she di ...
... one of those of the Plague in ...
... Circh ... visited this Summer
... of ... prudent Wom ...
... at Patience endured m ... Afflict ...
... H ... Parents had given her exc ...
... reeding and she was excellent at h ...
... which my Father being improved not ...
... in great stead. She was comp ...
... Divinity History and Poetry, and
... instilling into my Ears such
... tional Precepts as my younger
... pacity of. Nor did she ever fail
... Faith ... as adding Example Re ...
... Cures to boot. She was
... by ... of Note with
... a ... div ... m
... her Neighbours and ... a
... and ... John she was tru ...
...
...
...
... Name of those that we ...

then at the Lodge, Mr *Richard Penket Warden*
Mr *James Collier*, Mr *Richard Sankey*, Henry
Littler, *John Ellam*, *Richard Ellam*, and *Hugh*
Brewer

CE 25 I left *Co shire* and came to *London*
about the End of this Month *viz* the 30th
Day 4 *Hor* afterward About a Fortnight or
three Week before I came to *London*, Mr. *Jonas*
Moore brought and acquainted me with Mr
William Lily, it was on a *Friday* Night and
I think on the 23th of *Novem*

Dec 2 This Day at Noon I first became
acquainted with Mr *John Booker*

12 I was invited by Mrs *Marsh* to keep
my continuance with her at *Lim-House*, which I
did.

2 4 H 30 Minutes I went thither

16 *Feb* A Boyle broke out of my
Throat under my right Ear.

14 The Mathematical Feast was at the
White Hart in the *Old-Baily* where I dined.

Mar 1 I first moved the Lady *Mainwaring*,
in way of Marriage and received a fair Answer though no Cond sceration

Apr 2 I went to Sir *John Mainwaring's*,
with the Lady *Mainwaring*

May 28 I went towards *Bath*

2 Mr *Humphrey Stafford*
and I went into *Stafford's House*

Jun 12 I went from *Bytham* to *Englefield* and the
next Morning about 5 of the Clock I came to
the Home

14. I first became acquainted with Dr *Wim-berley*, Minister of *Englefield*, 3 *Hor. post merid.*

16, One *Hor. post merid* it pleased God to put me in Mind, that I was now placed in the Condition I always desired, which was, That I might be enabled to live to my self and Studies, without being forced to take Pains for a Livelihood in the World And seeing I am thus retired, according to my Heart's Desire, I beseech God to bless me in my Retirement, and to prosper my Studies that I may faithfully and diligently serve him, and in all Things submit to his Will, and for the Peace and Happiness I enjoy (in the Miss-of bad Times) to render him all humble Thanks and for what I attain to in the course of my Studies to give him the Glory

June 2. Eleven H— —m—d the L—w M—rn—g give n— —t l—n g —rm—h—d w—th —ack, wher—n was —hr —one —t—e Fr—

—

28 — —n 15 Minutes past merid. I fell ill and Ten — — 30 Minut— — —d, took my P—e I was p—ned in my Head, Reins Thighs, — —n—g a C— a Post— at Night and —v— g— —n it I men—ed

— — This Day I was much pained in my head and —

I — —arks —

— T — — M—rn— g entred upon h— — S—u— —

26. Ten *Hor. ante merid* I began to be fick, and 5 *Hor.* 15 Minutes *poſt merid.* I took my Bed, the Diſeaſe happened to be a violent Fever.

30 About 2 *Hor poſt merid* (as I was afterwards told) Mr *Humphry Stafford*, the Lady *Mainwaring's* ſecond Son (ſuſpecting I ſhould marry his Mother) broke into my Chamber, and had like to have killed me, but *Chriſtopher Smith* withheld him by Force, for which all Perſons exceedingly blamed him in Regard it was thought I was near Death and knew no Body God be bleſſed for this Deliverance.

Aug 1 I was in the Extremity of my Fever ſenſleſs and raging

12 Being ſomewhat mended of my Fever, I this Day got up About this Time the Lady *Mainwaring* fell into a Fever, and Captain *Wharton* had the Plague

25. Was the firſt Day I went down Stairs.

31. I was very faint and ill again

Septemb 2 I fell ill again and became light in my Head.

9 I took a Purge which wrought very well, and mended

28 I went to viſit the Lady *Mainwaring*.

Octob 26 I fell Sick of a Quartain Ague, at Mr *Staffords* having been Invited there to Dinner

Novemb 1 I went towards *London* and came thither the next Day by Noon

25 My Ague left me

The

30. The Lady *Mainwaring* came to Live at her House at *Bradfield*.

Dec. 16. Being much troubled with Phlegm, I took an Opening Drink from Dr. *Wharton*.

1648 *January* 14. I went towards *Bradfield* from *London*.

Feb. 25. I was very Ill as I went to *Theale*.

29 Very Sick in the Afternoon

March 2. Being at *Pangborne*, I was very Ill there

12. Captain *Wharton* taken in his Bed Two *Hor. ante Merid.* he was carried to *Newgate* Six *Hor. post Merid*

May 1.. I entertained *John Fox* into my Service

22 The Lady *Mainwaring* Sealed me a Lease of the Parks at *Bradfield*, worth —— per *Ann*.

June 6 Having entred upon the Study of Plants this Day, about Three of the Clock, was the first time I went a Simpling, Dr. *Carter* of *Reading*, and Mr *Watlington* an Apothecary there, accompanying me.

29 The Lady *Mainwaring* Sealed me a Lease of the Field Mead, worth 50 l per *Annum*

August 26 Captain *Wharton* made an Escape out of *Newgate*.

29 I began my Journey towards *Bristow*, with Mr *Hutchinson*.

31. We came to *Bristow*.

Sept 6. We returned to *Bradfield*

October 23 Going towards *London*, I was robb'd in *Maidenhead* Thicket 5 *Hor. post Merid*.

Nov. 3.

Nov. 6. Having several times before, made Application to the Lady *Mainwaring*, in way of Marriage, this Day, Eleven *Hor.* Seven Minutes *ante Merid.* She promised me not to Marry any Man, unless my self

10. Two *Hor.* Fifteen Minutes *post Merid.* She Sealed a Contract of Marriage to me.

15. I was Sequestred of my Lands in *Berkshire*

21 The Sequestration was taken off at *Reading.*

Decemb. 5. 1549 The Lady *Mainwaring* was Sequestred by the Committee of *Reading*, upon her Son *Humfrey Stafford's* Information.

Feb. 14. An Order for Receiving the Lady *Mainwarings* Rents

April 7 Eleven *Hor.* Thirty Minutes *ant. Merid.* I came to Mr *Watleton's* House to Table, who was an Apothecary in *Reading*, and a very good Botanist

25. My Journey to the Physick Garden in *Oxford.*

May 8 I was Godfather to *Elias Yardley* at *Reading*

June 3. This Afternoon I kissed the Duke of *Gloucester* and Lady *Elizabeth's* Hands, at Sion House.

Aug 1 The Astrologers Feast at *Painters-Hall*, where I Dined

Octob. 16 I accompanied the Lady *Mainwaring* to *London*

31 The Astrologers Feast.

Nov 16 Eight *Hor. ante Merid* I Married the Lady *Mainwaring* We were Married in *Silver-Street*, London.

20 I was Arrested by Mr *Ives* for my Brother *Mainwaring*'s Debt.

21 Captain *Wharton* was re-taken and carried to Prison

Decem 19 I agreed with Mr *Myne*, for Printing my *Fasciculus Chemicus*.

21 I first began to learn to diffect a Body

650 *Feb.* 18 I met Mr *Ives*, and we came to an Agreement.

June 3 Mr *Lilly* and my Self, went to visit Dr *Ardee*, at his House in the Minories

15 My self, my Wife, and Dr *Wharton* went to visit Mr. *John Tredefcant*, at *South-Lambeth*

21 I and my Wife went towards *Bradfield*.

22 Ten *Hor.* Thirty Minutes *ante Merid.* we arrived there

24 Mr *William Forster*, and his Lady came to Visit us.

25 I and Captain *Wharton* went to Visit him at *Rushall*

26. Nine *Hor.* Forty-two Minutes *post Meridiem* we Arrived at *Maulden*

July 2 Six *Hor. post Merid.* I was served with a Subpœna at Sir *Humfrey Forster*'s Suit.

Much Troubled with the Tooth Ach on the Right-side

8 Being at the Astrologers Feast, two Hor. &c. I was Chosen Steward for the following Year.

Captain

Captain *Wharton* having been carried to the *Gate-House* the 21st of *November* last, the next Day after, I went to Mr. *Lilly*, and acquainted him therewith, who professed himself very Sorry because he knew *Bradshaw* intended to hang him, and most generously (forgetting the Quarrel that had been between the Captain and him) promised me to use his Interest with Mr *B. de Whitert* (his Patron) to obtain his Release I thought it was prudent to have my Name then (as the Times stood) not to appear in Print as the Instrument that wrought Mr *Lilly* to do this Kindness for him, and therefore in Captain *Wrartons* Epistle to the Reader before his Almanack in 1651 Wherein his Publick Acknowledgments are made, of or Lu Aidance in this Strait, all Acknowledgment me are omitted tho' in Truth I was the only Person that moved and induced and often solicited Mr *Lilly* to perfect his Enlargement Having at all time for r n Luc n 1650 befriended Captain H not on' in discovering a Plot I h ard were laid against h m th se cr d wh ch a o oc r in my Purse freely and liberally owards s Support in many Necessitous Occations Upon Mr Lilly s applica t on Mr the uth he advised hat the Capa n had hie q n n were ig e least Co plent and after whe h being bri n v o ly ft big no m ur o of i va a ne Wea Ch r an

an

man to the Council of State, Mr. *Lilly* having
also by this time, made some other of the
said Council, the Captain's Friends (upon his
Petition) he was discharged, no other Engage-
ment being taken from him, but that he
would not thence forward write against the
Parliament or State Hereupon he became
utterly void of all Subsistance (which whilst
he was under Troubles, some or other contri-
buted unto besides what he got by Writing
against those Times) and thereupon, consulting
with me about a new Course of Life, and how
he might subsist, I frankly offered him my
House at Bradfild in Berks for him, his Wife
and Family to live at with some other Ad-
int as there, which he most gladly and
thankfuly accepting he went thither, and
past his Time with Quiet and Comfort for
the most part till his Majesty was restored to
his Crown, and hereupon he stiled me in his
Almanack for the Year 1653, his *Oaken Friend*.

I bought of Mr. Mohun all his
Books and Mathematical Instruments

Light For Thirty Minutes past Noon.
I bought Mr. Twyne's Books

I put in a Plea and Demur to
Court Freeres Bill

Mrs. Catherine Burgess Street only
answer to my Uncle Anthony Burgess, was
born

I agreed with Mr. Luster for his House
where I afterwards dwelt

23 Two *Hor. post Merid.* he Sealed me a Leafe of the faid Houfe at 44 *l per Ann.*

26. *Post Merid.* I came thither to dwell.

1651. *Jan.* 1 I fell into a great Loosenefs, which turned into a Fever, but mended next Day

7 Captain *Wharton* returned from *Bradfeild,* whether I fent him to receive my Rents.

16. Four *Hor. post Merid.* my Demurrer againft Sir *Humfrey Forster's* Bill was argued and held good

22 About this time my left fide of my Neck began to break forth, occafioned by Shaving my Beard with a bad Razor.

27. About this time I grew Melancholly and Dull, and heavy in my Limbs and Back

About this Time I began to learn Sealgraving, Cafting in Sand, and Goldfmiths Work.

Feb. 1 Three *Hor* Thirty Minutes *post Merid* I agreed with Mrs *Backhoufe* of *London,* for her deceaf'd Hufbands Books.

March 7, I went to *Maidstone* with Dr. *Child* the Phyfician And three *Hor post Merid* I firft became acquainted with Dr *Flood.*

18 This Night my Maid s Bed was on Fire, but I rofe quickly (and Thanks to God) quenched it

April 3 *Post Merid* Mr *William Backhoufe* of *Swallowfield* in *Com Berks,* caufed me to Call him Father thence forward

25 Five *H* Thirty Minutes *post Merid.* my Father *Backhoufe* brought me acquainted

with

with the Lord *Ruthin*, who was a most Inge
mou Person.

June 10. Mr. *Backhouse* told me I must
now needs be his Son because he had commu
nicated so many Secrets to me

July 2. I gave Mr *Grismond* my *Theatrum
Chymicum Britannicum* to Print.

Aug 1. Captain *Wharton* went to receive
my Rents at *Bradfield*

Aug 14. The Astrologers Feast at *Painter.
Hall, London.*

This Night about one of the Clock, I fell
Ill of a Surfeit, occasioned by Drinking Wa
ter after Venison. I was greatly oppressed in
my Stomach, and next Day Mr. *Saunders* the
Astrologian sent me a piece of Briony Root to
hold in my Hand and within a quarter of an
Hour, my Stomach was freed of that great
Oppression, which nothing which I took from
Dr *Wharton* could do before

About this Time my Brother *Peter Mainwa
ring's* Wife dyed

Sept 1 Captain *Wharton* went to receive
my Rent

Mr. *Vaughan* began to engrave the Pi
ctures in *Norton's Ordinal* he wrought and fi
nished all the Cuts for my *Theatrum Chymicum*
here at my House in *Black-Fryers*

Captain *Fletcher* Arrested, and Mr *Grif*
Bail

Sept 3 My Father *Backhouse* and I went
to Mr *Graves*, the great Botanist, at Pe-

. Mr *Lilly* gave me several old Astrolo-
gical Manuscripts

. . About Four *pm Merid* my Wives
eldest Son M *Edward Stafford*, died

. Ten *r C Merid* he was buried in *Brad-
f* Church

. . Sir *John Backhouse* of *Swallowfield*, his
Widdow died

D *m* . Two . . . . Dr *Page*
lent me several Chymical Manuscr p and here
began my Acquaintance with him

. I sent Captain *Aku* to receive my
Rents at *Bradfi*

1652 Jul 2 The Gum at the back end
of the Right side of my upper Jaw cleft, and
about Nine *H pm Merid* I felt a new
Tooth coming up

2 Sx h p G Mer the first Copy of
y The . . an Bo ham was sold to
the Earl of *. .*

. Th . . . M *Mr Lilly* gave
ne hi P . . Colours of which there
. . had been C . . n

. T . Forty five Minutes p
. Satu . . and Mr *S gf s*
Co . . . L a of my Wives Join-
. . . by . re . . of
. . . . I . . d b n
. . . .

. . . Hebr .
.

. . . . . Ash and a
C . . . .

... Six How Fifteen Minutes ... Mer ...
Dr ... let me Blood

... This Morning my Father Ba... ... ope...
... his ... ery freely touching the great
...

... I paid my Man ... For his Wages,
... ... ged him of my Service

... This Morning I received more Satisfa...
... ... Father ... ... on the Qu...
... I ... ...d

... Captain ... ... to receive

... I went to the Sessions at N... where
... ... Governour of ... ... In...
... on by Sir Pumfry ... ... was exceed...
... ... to the wonder of the
... Court

... The Inquisition upon my Statute
... Pounds was found at Maidenhead

... my Wife Tabled this Summer at
... ...

... Hot ... ... Dr Whitby
... ... came to visit me at ... ... s,
... the first time I faw the Doctor

Captain When h was sent to receive my
... ... to... brought his Wife and ...
... ...

... ... to ... ... Assizes to hear
... Tryed and took ... ...

... ... towards ... ...
... ... Sick of a violent and
... ... about Noon

D ...

... I arrived at *Gawsworth*, where my Father in Law Mr *Mainwaring* then lived.

Sept 11 Young *John Tredescant* dyed

16 He was buried in *Lambeth* Church Yard by his Grandfather

23 I took a Journey into the *Peak*, in search of Plants and other Curiosities,

27 I came to Mr *Jo Tomison's*, who dwelt near *Dove Edge*, he used a Call, and had Responses in a soft Voice He told me Dr *Wharton* was Recovering from his Sickness, and so it proved

Octob 2 I came to *Litchfield*

3 Mr *Anthony Dugdale* moved me to refer Controversy between me and my Uncle *Thomas Ashmole*

My said Uncle quitted his Title to me, which pretended to my House in *Litchfield*, and Sealed to me a Deed of Bargain and Sale

14. He also Sealed me a Release, and gave me Possession.

Nov 2. Four *Hor. post Merid* I returned to *London* and in an Hour after to my House.

3 Mr *Lilly* called before the Committee of plundred Ministers and committed

20 My Wife went again to Mr *Tredescant's*, to stay some time there

21 I discharged my Man *Hobs* of my Service

Decemb — I was served with a *Subpœna* at Sr *Humfrey Forsters* Suit Three *Hor* Forty Minutes *post Merid*

15 His Bill was filed

M)

18 My Sister Mrs. *Dorothy Mainwaring* came to live with my Wife Eleven Hor. ante Merid.

She stayed with her but till the 16th of *Janu* y following.

Jan. 13. 1653 I held a Court at *Bradfield*, as Lord of that Mannor.

Mr *Anthony Brook* of *Sunning* was my Steward, Sir *Humfrey Forster* coming thither, I Arrested him

1 My Wife left Mr. *Tradescant's*, and came to Mr *Fum's*

&c 18 The Astrologers Feast was held.

&c Dr *Langbaine*, Provost of Queens College shewed me Mr. *Seldens* Letter to him, wherein he said, he should be glad to be acquainted with me, for he found by what I had Published, that I was affected to the furtherance of all good Learning

This Morning I first became acquainted with *Arise Evans*, a *Welch* Prophet, and speaking of the Parliament, I asked him when it would end? He answered, the time was short, and it was even at the door, this very Morning at Eleven of the Clock, the Mace was taken away from the Speaker, and the Parliament dissolved, and I conjecture it was much about the time that *Arise Evans* and I had this Discourse

May 2. Three Hor. post Merid. My Cousin *William Humble* came to *London* He went to Mr *Gy* upon Tryal

2 My Father *Backhouse* lying Sick in *Fleetstreet*, against St *Dunstans* Church, and not

not knowing whether he should live or dye, about Eleven of the Clock, told me in Syllables, the true Matter of the Philosophers Stone, which he bequeathed to me as a Legacy

June 21. I agreed with Dr. *Bathurst* for the remaining Years, in my House at *Black-Fryers*.

July 25. Nine *Hor*. Thirty Minutes, I was first acquainted with Mr. *Selden*, who used me very Courteously, and encouraged me in my Studies.

Aug. 8 Eight *Hor* Thirty Minutes *ante Merid* I began my Voyage with Dr *Carver* into *Cornwall*, he going thither to open a Mine for for the Lord *Mobun*

17 Nine *Hor post Merid* we came to *Bre knock*

Sept 12 Nine *hor* Fifteen Minutes *post Merid*. we returned to *London*

Octob 1. Seven *Hor post Merid* I first became acquainted with Mr *Ogilby*.

4. I was troubled with the Tooth ach, Major *Ruswell*, (Dr. *Bathurst*'s Apothecary) stopped it.

16 Sir *John Heydon*, Lieutenant of the Ordnance to King *Charles* the 1st, and my worthy Friend dyed

Nov 18 My Aunt *Bowyer* Wife to my Uncle *Anthony Bowyer* was buried

20 I was again troubled with the Tooth Ach for three Days.

23. My good Friend and Neighbour Dr. *Wimberley*, Minister of *Englefield* in *Berkshire*, dyed

25. He

25. He was buried at St. *Margaret's* in *Weſt-minſter*, where formerly he had been Parſon.

This Day I bound my Couſin *William Aſhmole* an Apprentice to Mr. *Clothier*, a Sadler

1554. *Jan* 21. Doctor *Wharton* began his Lecture at the Phyſitian's College 10 *Hor. inte merid*

Feb 6 The Hearing in Chancery, (came on) wherein Sir *Humphrey Forſter* was Plantiff againſt me As ſoon as my Anſwer was opened it was referred to Mr. *Chaloner Chute* my Counſel to determine.

Mar 11 4 *Hor poſt merid* Mr *Chute* ſigned his Award

16 In Purſuance whereof I received from Sir *Humphrey Forſter* 350 *l.* 11 *Hor. ant. merid.*

Feb 2 I acquainted Doctor *Wharton* with my Secret for the Cure of the *Iliaca Paſſio*, and he applied it this Morning to Mr *Faithorne* the Graver, and it cured him

July 2 My Wife went to lodge at Mr *Wits.*

17 I came to *Litchfield*

22 I returned thence.

Aug 22 Aſtrologer's Feaſt.

24. I made a Journey to *Canterbury, Dover*, &c.

Sept 1 I returned to *London.*

15 I went to viſit Mr. *Oughtred*, the famous Mathematician

28 I received 300 Pounds from Sir *Humphry Forſter*

Oct 7. Mr. *William Floyd's* firſt Wife (was) buried at *Swallowfield* in *Barkſhire.*

Nov. 24. 6 *Hor. poſt Merid.* my good Father-in-Law Mr. *Peter Mainwaring* died at *Gawſworth.*

Dec. 8 Doctor *Pordage* was put out of *Bradfield* Living By his Removal it fell to me to preſent, and knowing the Worth and Learning of Mr *Floyd* (then living with my Father *Backhouſe* as Tutor to his Children) I reſolved to beſtow it upon him and thereupon ſent for him up to *London* and on the 18*th* acquainted him with my Intention

3o. I ſigned a Preſentation to him, he was examined by the Tryers, and paſſed with Approbation But Deſigns being laid againſt him by Mr *Fowler* and Mr *Ford* both Miniſters of *Reading* who endeavoured to bring in Doctor *Temple* ſuppoſing Sir *Humphry Fiſter* had a Right of Preſentation he thought better to reſign his Preſentation to me than to undergo a Conteſt with thoſe Men

1655 *Mar* 3o Hereupon I preſented one Mr *Adams* who having a Living of 110 *l. per Ann* and finding he muſt undergo a Conteſt with thoſe that oppoſed Mr *Floyd* thought fitter to keep his own Living than part with it in hopes of a far better

Ap. 29 The Peace between *England* and *France* was proclaimed at *Weſtminſter* 10 Hor. 45 Minutes to Mr. ria

1654 And at 11 Hor. 45 Minutes it was proclaimed at *St. Paul's*

Apr 1 Archbiſhop of *Armagh* (was) buried

May

May 23. First Show at Sir *William Davenant's* Opera

June 26. I fell sick, and had a great Loose-

July In this Month I was troubled with a great Pain in my right Breast.

I paid Mr *Faithorne* 7 *l.* for engraving my Picture.

August 1 Journey to Mr *Sterill's* in *Essex*

Colonel *Wharton* came home upon his Parole

2. I signed and sealed my Presentation for *Breasfield* Living to Mr. *Lancelot Smith* 6 Hor. Minutes *arte Merid* and delivered it to the Committee

The Man, after some Contest, enjoyed the Living, and the Right of Presentation being acknowledged to be mine, I had no farther Trouble.

This Day the Astrologer's Feast was held.

4 Cousin —— *Thompson* (was) christened

I went toward *Litchfield.*

About 9 *Hor ante merid* I came first to Mr *Dugdales* at *Blyth-Hall*

I returned to *London*

I went towards *Blyth-Hall.*

Jan 14 10 Hor. 40 Minutes *ante Me-*rid I returned to *London*

22 My Cousin *Everard Mainwaring* died.

I went towards *Blyth-Hall.*

5 Hor. *post merid* I bruised my Toe with the Fall of a great Form.

May

May 2, 7 Hor c c Merid I returned to
L do

15 I acc mpanied Mr Dugda'e in his Jour-
n   to a   th F rs E r 30 Minutes or
M re

7   3   H r   Minutes after nerd we
came to o

      H e Minutes   em d I re-
t rne to L d

S r 2   I te ill of the Tooth-ach, which
con in a T r Day

o8 8 The Cause between me and my Wife
was heard where Mr Serjeant Maynard observed
to the Court that there were 800 Sheets of
Depositions on my Wife's Part and not one
Word proved against me of using her ill, or
ever giving her a bad or provoking Word

9 The Lord Commissioners having found
no Cause for allowing my Wife Alimoney,
did at H   afterward deliver my Wife to me,
whereupon I carried her to Mr Lilly's and
thereupon I   s both

           Minutes p ß Merid I
was admit to   d   Tim

I   A   at H   20 Minutes po 7
   Th ndered and Lightened and at the
Tme was the Writ Sald for Summons of
th n   Lords of the Parliament

2   I went my Wife came towards him

2   I went to L

       I advanced towards Buy H ll

1668   I came to Bedford

5   I returned to Woy

31

Mar 30 I dined with the *Florida* Embassa-
dir at Mr *Martin Noell's*

May 7 I first went to the Record-Office in
the Tower, to collect Materials for my Work
on the Garter.

I was struck by a Coach-Horse, on the
inside of my left Thigh

June 12. I first became acquainted with Sir
... *Trusden*

July 7 1 *Hor. post merid* I went towards
.... and *Staffordshire* In this Journey
visited Sir *Thomas Leigh* Sir *Harvy Bagot*, Sir
.... and the Earl of *Denbigh*.

I returned to *London*

.... I was entred into Mr *Henshaw's*
.... in the *Middle Temple*, which I bought
.... for *130l* being admitted to it this
.... 30 Minutes *ante merid*

.... 15 Minutes *ante Merid* I
.... my Goods thither, and 2 *Hor. post*
came the rest.

.... 24 I became acquainted with
....

I went to *Windsor* and took Mr. *Hollar's*
.... Views of the Castle
was at the Artillaries Feast

I came to *Barnes*, to table

.... broken up by the Sol-
.... of searching for the King,
.... going out of it

.... *Hethington*, an Apothecary
.... an able Botanist (my very
....

5. Mr. *Lilly* received a gold Chain from the King of *Sweden*.

Nov. 2 Was the Astrologer's Feast.

Dec. 12 Mr *Tredescant* and his Wife told me they had been long considering upon whom to bestow their Closet of Curiosities when they died, and at last had resolved to give it unto me.

14. This Afternoon they gave their Scriviner Instructions to draw a Deed of Gift of the said Closet to me.

16 5 *Hor* 30 Minutes *post merid*. Mr. *Tredescant* and his Wife sealed and delivered to me the Deed of Gift of all his Rarities

1650 *Jan.* 3 My Uncle *Anthony Bowyer* died

Mar. 2. I went into *Warwickshire*

Apr 11 I returned to *London*

June 6. 4 *Hor.* 15 Minutes *post merid* I first became acquainted with Sir *Edward Walker* Garter.

16 4 *Hor* *post merid* I first kissed the King's Hand, being introduced by Mr *Thomas Chiffinch*

18 10 *Hor* *ante merid* was the second Time I had the Honour to discourse with the King and then he gave me the Place of *Windsor* Herald

2. This Day the Warrant bears Date

About this Time the King appointed me to make a Description of his Medals and I had then delivered into my Hands and *Henry* the VIIIth's Closet assigned for my Use.

July

Aug 19. This Morning Mr. Secretary *Morie*
told me that the King had a great Kindness
for me.

Aug 6 Mr *Ayton*, the King's chief Gentle-
man-Usher came to me into the Closet, and
told me the King had commanded that I
should have my Diet at the Waiters Table,
which I accordingly had.

10 The Officers at Arms took the Oaths,
and my self among them, as *Windsor* Herald.

14 This Afternoon was the first publick
Meeting of the Officers at Arms in the Heralds Office.

21 I presented the King with the Three
Books I had printed, *viz. Fasciculus Chemicus,*
Theatrum Chemicum, and *The Way to Bliss*

Sept 3. My Warrant signed for the Comptroler's Office in the Excise.

5 I delivered my said Warrant for the
Excise to the Commissioners of Appeals

24 5 *Hor. post mer d.* I came to the
Excise Office and took Possession of the Com-
ptrolers Office.

2 I was this Night called to the Bar
in *Middle Temple* Hall.

I had my Admittance to the Bar in the
said Hall.

28 I took my Oath, as Comptroler of
Excise, before Baron *Turner.*

15 I was admitted a Member
of Royal Society at *Gresham-College.*

A Warrant was signed by the King
being Secretary of *Surinam* in the *W. R-*

E   *Apr.*

Apr 3 My Patent for Comptrolership of the Excise bears Test

13. The King gave my Lord Chamberlain Order, to settle me as the first Herald, in case any Dispute should happen

May 16 The Grant of Arms to me from Sir *Edward Bysh Clarencieux* bears Date

June 29 *John Walsh* was sworn my Deputy.

Nov 6 Mr *Thomas Chiffinch* dined at my Chamber in the *Midale Temple*

July 12. I christened Mr *Buttler* the Goldsmith's Son, *William*

1662 *Jan* 26 I paid in 50 *l* the Half of my Royal Present to the King.

Mar 5 I sent a Set of Services and Anthems to *Litchfield* Cathedral, which cost me 16 *l*.

Apr. 22. Mr *John Tredescant* died

May 29. I was made one of the Commissioners for recovering the King's Goods

May 30 My Father *Backhouse* died this Evening at *Swallowfield*

This *Easter-Term* I preferred a Bill in *Chancery* against Mrs *Tredescant*, for the Rarities her Husband had settled on me

June 17 About 3 Her *post merid* The Commissioners for the Office of Earl-Marshal first sat in *Whitehall*

This Afternoon my Father *Backhouse* was buried in *Swallowfield* Church

29 11 her 30 Minutes *ante merid* I first kissed the Queen's Hand

Aug I accompanied Mr *Dugdale* in his Visitation of *Derby* and *Nottinghamshire*

6 I bought Mr. *Tamepemines* Interest in the Lease of *Herrich* Lands

Sept. I paid the other half of my Royal Present to the King, *viz* 50 *l*

Dec. 5 I christened Captain *Wharton's* Daughter *Ann*

563 *Mar* I accompanied Mr *Dugdale* in his Visitation of *Staffordshire* and *Derbyshire,*

Mar. Towards the End of this Month I christened Mr *Timothy Emar's* Son of *Windsor.*

27 I fell ill of a feverish Distemper

July 6 I went towards *Oxford* attending the Body of Archbishop *Juxon.*

Aug 3. 9 Hor. ante merid I began my Journey to accompany Mr *Dugdale* in his Visitations of *Shropshire* and *Cheshire.*

Oct 10 I returned to *London*

Nov 21 Mr *Povey* brought the Earl of *Peterborough* to my Chamber

1564 *Jan* 19 Mr. *Thomas* first promised me a Place in the White-Office

Feb 5 The Benchers of the *Middle Temple* granted me an Assignment of my Chamber in the *Middle Temple*

8 My Picture was drawn by Mr *Le Neve* in my Heralds-Coat

12 Mr *Dugdale* fell sick of a Fever,

13 I gave 20 *l* towards the Repair of *Litchfield* Minster

Mar 17 I Christened *Secundus* Son to Mr *Lacy* the Comedian

May 18. My Cause came to hearing in *Chancery* against Mrs. *Tredescant.*

June

... gave ... Volumes of Mr *Dug-*
... Work to the ... Library, and had
the Acknowledgment.

... dic *Junii* 1654.

... Mr *Ashmole* of the utter *Bar* bare
... for the Books now presented
... by him for the Library

... The White Office was opened, wherein
I was Comptroller

... Having bought the Third Part of
... Chamber upon the Death of Mr. *Jerrot*, the
... his Daughter gave me an Assignment of it

... at the Reading in the
Middle T... whereat I was one of the Stewards

1654 ... About 8 ... antedated Mr
Thomas ... gave a Warrant of Attorney to con-
fess a Judgment to me of 1200 *l*

... S ... a byn sealed his Deputation to
me for visiting B... shire

M... I began to make my Visitation of
Berkshire at *Reading*

Aug ... I went towards *Blyth-Hall*

This Year about 5 of *July* (the Plague en-
creasing) I retired to *Roe-Barns*, and the following Winter composed a good Part of my
Work of the *Garter* there.

1656 *Jn...* I bestowed on the Bailiffs of
Litchfield a large chased Silver Bowl and Cover,
which cost me ... 3 s. 6 d

June

June I presented the publick Library at *Ox-ford* with Three Folio Volumes, containing a Description of the Consular and Imperial Coines there, which I had formerly made and digested, being all fairly transcribed with my own Hand. In Acknowledgment of which the following was entred in the Register of Bene-factors

Elias Ashmole *armiger,* & *Regius Fecialis de* Windesore, *vir præstantissimus & rei antiquariæ peritissimus, accuratissimum antiquorum Numismatum Laudentium Catalogum in tria Volumina distributum concinnavit & Bibliothecæ Bodleianæ dono dedit*

Aug This Month I went to *Byth-Hall,* and returned the same Month

Sept 2 The dreadful Fire of *London* began

Oct 4 1 Hor 30 Minutes *post merid* some of my Books carried to my Cousin *Moyse's,* were returned to my Chamber at the *Temple.*

11 1 Hor 30 Minutes *post merid,* my first boatful of Books, which were carried to Mrs. *Tradescant's* the 3d of *September,* were brought back to the *Temple*

18 1 *post merid* all the rest of my Things, were brought thence to the *Temple*

1667 *May* I bought Mr *John Booker's* Study of his and gave 140*l* for them

July 16 I went to *Warwickshire*

24 I returned to *London*

31 I went again towards *Warwickshire.*

Aug 21 I returned to *Roe-Barnes*

Nov. 25 I took a Lease of the *Mygges* in

Litchfield from the Bailiffs, and this Day paid 20*l* part of 40*l* Fine

1668. *Jan.* 11 I paid to Mr *Rawlins* 20*l.* the remaining Part of my Fine for the *Moggs* at *Litchfield*

Apr. 1 2 Hor. *ante merid.* the Lady *Mainwaring*, my Wife, died

25 Mr *Joseph Williamson* and Dr. *Thomas Smith* (afterwards Bishop of *Carlisle*) dined with me at my Chamber in the *Temple*

June 9 5 Hor *post merid.* the Lords Commissioners of the Treasury appointed me to execute the Office of Accomptant-General in the Excise and Country Accomptant

6 6 Hor *post merid.* they appointed me to execute the Place of Country- Accomptant in the Excise.

Aug 10 I went towards *Blyth-Hall.*

25 I returned to *London*

Sept 4 7 Hor 30 Minutes *ante merid.* I concluded with Mr *Lawrence*, for his House in *Sheere-Lane.* At 7 Hor *post merid* he sealed his Assignment to me

15 Doctor *Currer* the Chymical Physitian, my most entire Friend, died

Oct 1 He was buried at St *Clement Danes*, and Dr *William Ford* preached his Funeral-Sermon *November* 1

Nov 2 I married Mrs *Elizabeth Dugdale* Daughter to *William Dugdale*, Esq, *Norroy* King of Arms at *Lincoln's-Inn* Chappel Dr. *William Boyd* married us, and her Father gave her. The Wedding was finished at 10 Hor *post merid*

Dec.

Dec. 3. Doctor *William Floyd* married.

29 *Justinian Pagitt*, Esq, died.

1569 *Jan.* 2. Mr. *Just. Pagitt* was buried at St *Giles*'s in the Fields.

April 15 Mr. *Rose*, the King's Gardiner, and my self, went to Mrs. *Tredescants*, and thence to Captain *Forsters* at *South-Lambeth*, where I first was acquainted with him.

17. Mr. *Oldenburgh* (Secretary to the Royal Society) sent me a Letter, that Count *Magalotti* would visit me at my Chamber, from the Prince of *Tuscany*

19 Count *Magalotti* and two other Gentlemen of the Prince of *Tuscany*'s chief Attendants, came to my Chamber to see my Library and Coins

27 I felt the first Touch of the Gout, in my great Toe, on my left Foot, and in my left Fore-finger

June 5. I and my Wife went to *Horsham* to visit Mr *Lilly*

9 We returned to *London*

July 6 I went towards *Oxford*

The Possession of the Theatre (built by Dr *Sheldon* Archbishop of *Canterbury*) was taken by the Vice-Chancellor

I received the Honour of being made a Doctor of Physick at *Oxford*.

Aug 11 I and my Wife went again to Mr *Lilly*'s.

22 Sir *William Backhouse* of *Swallowfield* dyed.

Sept 3 I returned to *London* from Mr *Lilly*'s.

Mrs. *Doris Pagitt*, Wife to *Justinian Pagitt* Esq; was buried.

21. I went towards *Swallowfield* to serve at the Funeral of Sir *William Backhouse*

28. He was buried at *Swallowfield*.

29 I Let a Leafe of *Hometich* Lands to *H. Aldrich* for feven Years

Novemb 3 This Evening Dr. *Yates*, Principal of *Brazen-Nofe* Colledge, prefented me with a *Diploma* from the Univerfity of *Oxford*, for my Degree of Doctor of Phyfick between fix and Seven at Night

About the middle of *December*, my Friendfhip began to be renewed with Dr *Wharton* which had been difcontinued for many Years by reafon of his unhandfome and unfriendly dealing with me

1670. *March* 14 I beftowed a Grave-Stone on Mr *Booker* formerly, and this Day paid for it, it had this Infcription in Capital Letters.

Ne oblivione contereretur Urna

Iohannis Bookeri Aftrologi

qui fat ceffit

VI o *Idus* Aprilis Anno Chrifti Juliano

MDCLXVII.

Hoc ill. p fui amoris Monumentum

Elias Afhmole

Armiger

.. I was entertained by Monfieur *Lionberg* the *wedyn* Envoy

31. I obtained the Kings Warrant to my Book of the *Garte*.

May 5. The Earl of *Anglesea* visited me at my Chamber in the Temple

  ~ I Dined at Sir *Charles Cotterels* with the *French* Envoy, and after Dinner they went to my Chamber in the Temple, where I so satisfied the Envoy touching the King of *Sweden's* Precedence in the Order before his Masters, that he thereupon waved the further Prosecution of that Affair

  June 22 Captain *Burgh*, my old Acquaintance, dyed

  July 5 The Lord *Hatton*, my much Honoured Friend dyed this Morning

  I fell ill of a Surfeit, but Thanks be to God, Recovered the next Day.

  I Dined with the *Swedish* Envoy.

  27 Sir *Gilbert Talbot*, Master of the Jewel House and Mr *Joseph Williamson* Dined at my Chamber in the Temple.

  August 19. Six *Hor. post merid.* my Cousin Whyte of *Totenham*, dyed

  My self and Wife went to Captain Burghs, at *Greenwich*.

  Sept 25 Eleven *Hor* 30 Minutes *ante merid* I became acquainted with the Count *de Mon-* Envoy from the Duke of *Savoy*

  Octob 8. I moved my Lord Archbishop of *Canterbury* for a License for Mr *Lilly*, to practise Physick, which he granted

  18 I fell Ill of the Gout, in my great Toe on the Right Foot

  I bled with Leeches, and was Well the next Morning

1671. *Jan.* 9 My Sister *Dugdale* dyed.

March 13 I became acquainted with Mr *Peter Arnold* the Chymist

April 4. My Brother *Dugdale* Married to Mrs. *Pigeon*

May 16 I Let a Lease of my House in *Litchfield*, to Mr *Edmund Falkingham*, for 7 Years.

July 20 I went towards *Blyth-Hall* with my Wife

31. I came to *Litchfield*

Aug 10 I and my Wife went to *Litchfield* where we were entertained by the Barliffs at a Dinner, and a great Banquet

15 We went to the Earl of *Denbigh* at *A wnker*.

18 Four *Hor. post Merid* I arrived at *London*.

Sept. 21 I went again towards *Blyth-Hall*

Octob. 5. I came to *Litchfield*, where I met my Brother *Mainwaring*

16 I and my Wife returned to *London*.

19 My Brother *Mainwaring* came to *London*

Decemb ~ My Brother *Mainwaring* took his Oath, as one of my Deputies. so did Mr *Tr t*

1672 *Ja 22* I was Entertained at Dinner by the *Venetian* Agent

May 2 Two *Hor* 40 Minutes, (*post merid*) I presented my Book of the *Gar* to the King

July 20 I and my Wife went to Mr *Lilly*, where we stayed till *September* the 2d.

Aug 20 My good Friend Mr *Wale*, sent me Dr *Dee*s Original Book and Papers

Sept 14 The Earl of *Peterborough* having about *June*, by the Duke of *York*'s Command, called

called at my Chamber in the *Temple*, for one of my Books of the *Garter*, to carry to the Duke, then at Sea, the Duke Received it with much Pleasure, and (*the Earl*) believed he had Read it all over.

27. Mr. *Philip Floyd's* Patent paffed the great Seal for the Reverfion of my Office of Comptroller of the Excife.

Octob. 12. Ten *Hor.* 30 Minutes *ante merid.* I Sprained my Right Foot.

17. The Earl of *Peterborough* prefented me to the Duke of *York*, who told me he had Read a great part of my Book, that I had done a great deal of Honour to *the Order of the Garter* that I had taken a great deal of Pains therein, and deferved Incouragement 9. *Hor.* 40 Minutes *ante Merid.*

Decemb. 17. Being at the Treafury Chamber, the Lord Treafurer *Clifford*, very Courteoufly invited me to his Lodgings in the Court.

20 I waited on him, and was received with great Kindnefs.

23 The Earl of *Briftol* gave great Commendations of my Book, and faid, he thought the *Knights of the Garter* were obliged to prefent me with fome confiderable Gift, and that himfelf would move it.

1673 *Jan.* 11 This Evening I fat with the Lord Treafurer two Hours.

27 Ten *Hor* 40 Minutes *ante Merid.* the Earl of *Bedford* gave his Approbation, with great Commendation of my Book of the Garter

Feb 3. Ten *Hor.* 30 Minutes *ante meria.* I delivered my Petition to the Earl of *Arlington*, for the Cuftom of Paper. with a defire of his Opinion about it· He anfwered, it was but a reafonable Requeft, and he would confer with the Lord Treafurer about it, before he moved the King and that he would do me Service.

13. Eight *Hor* 20 Minutes *poft merid.* I moved the Lord Treafurer for my Arrears of my Penfion, as *Windfor* Herald, and to favour my Petition for getting the Cuftom of fome Paper. The firft he faid fhould be done, and to the fecond, he would be my Friend, and fo he was.

March 13. My Book of *the Garter* was fent to Captain *Bartie* to be prefented to the King of *Denmark.*

16. I grew indifpofed with a Fulnefs in my Stomach, but taking fome Phyfick, I grew well

25 The Earl of *Denbigh* came to my Houfe to vifit me.

April 2 Seven *Hor poft merid* coming from *Windfor* in a Coach with Sir *Edward Walker*, the Coach overturned, and I Sprained my left Wrift.

17 I delivered my Book of the *Garter* to Sir *John Finch*, to Prefent it to the Duke of *Tufcany*

May 21 I received the Lord Treafurer's Warrant for 106 Pound, 13 Shillings and four-pence the Arrears of my Penfion

June 18

June 18 I received my Privy-Seal for 400 Pounds out of the Custom of Paper, which the King was pleased to bestow upon me, for my Work of the *Garter*

20 I was let Blood.

Jul 4. The Learned and Ingenious Sir *Robert Murray* dyed.

Sept. 29 I renewed my Lease of *Homer ch* Land, from the Vicars of *Litchfield*.

Octob. 4. I and my Wife came from *Horsham* to *London*, having spent a good part of the Summer with Mr *Lilly*

12 The Lady *Forster*, Sir *Humfrey Forster's* Widdow, dyed

Novemb. 8. This Morning Dr *Wharton* was found almost Dead in his Bed of an Apoplexy, and Palsy on his left side

12 He sent for me at Midnight, and because some Differences had formerly fallen out between us, he desired to be reconciled to me, which he was

15 Ten Ho. 15 Minutes *ante merid.* Dr *Wharton* dyed, and was buried in *Basinghall* Church in a Vault.

Decemb. 3 Dr. *Teme* the Physician, dyed this Evening He was buried at St *Andrews Undershaft* the seventh of *January* following.

1674 F/ 25 Nine Hor. 30 Minutes *ante merid.* I desired Mr. *Hayes*, the Earl Marshal's Secretary, to move his Lord, to give me leave to Resign my Heralds Place.

April 2. The Earl Marshal came to see my Chamber in the *Tower*

13 He gave me a *George* in Gold, which his Grandfather wore, when he went Embaſſador into *Germany*.

24 My Wife and I went to Mr *Lilly's*, where we ſtayed till 8 *September* following.

May 29. About Five *poſt merid* the Order was made in the Chapter Houſe at *Windſor*, for Recommending me to the Knights of the Garter

Jun. 20 I Dined with the Duke of *Lauderdale* at *Ham*, whither he had Invited me, and Treated me very kindly.

July 1 Sir *John Davis*, ſometime of *Panhne* in *Barkſhire*, dyed

20 I met with Mr *Thomas Henſhaw* upon his Return from *Denmark*, having brought me a Gold Chain and that King's Medal thereat, from the ſaid King

27. I firſt ſpake with the Prince Elector of *Brandenburgh's* Envoy

Auguſt 1 I lent Mr *Edward Hopkins* 400 Pounds, upon a Mortgage of his Lands in *Little Pry* near *Lichfield*

Sir *William Swan*, the King's Reſident at *Hamburgh* gave me an Account of his ſending my Books of the Garter to the Duke of *Saxony*, and Prince Elector of *Brandenburgh*, and gave me a Letter from the ſaid Prince

I waited on the King and ſhewed him the Gold Chain the King of *Denmark* ſent me, he liked it well, and gave me leave to wear it

October 2 Eleven *Hor.* 30 Minutes *ante merid.*
I and my Wife first entred my House at *South-Lambeth*

This Night Mr *Tredescant* was in danger of being robbed, but most strangely prevented.

28 I waited on the Earl Marshal to gain his Leave for disposing of my Heralds Place He told me I was a Person of that Ability, that he was loath to leave me, and put off the Discourse to a further time.

Novemb. 17 I received a Case of Excellent Pistols and a Silver Hilt for a Sword sent me as a Present, from the Earl of *Castlemaine*, from *Liege*.

26 Mrs *Tredescant* being willing to deliver up the Rarities to me, I carried several of them to my House

Decemb. 1 I began to remove the rest of the Rarities to my House at *South-Lambeth.*

2 This Night my Affair about the inlargeing my Control upon the Counties, was settled

18 Mr *Lilly* fell Sick, and was Let Blood in the Left Foot, a little above the Ancle, New Moon the Day before, and the Sun Eclipsed

20 Mr *Lilly* had a great Pain in his Left Leg, which lasted 24 Hours, and put him into a great Feaver

23 My Wife went to see him

25 I went to visit him also.

28. The Humour being fixed in two places upon his top of the Left Foot (one being the

F 2   place

place he was Let Blood in) and now grown ripe, they were launced by Mr Agar, an Apothecary (and no less a good Chirurgeon) of Kingston, after which he began to be at more Ease and the Feaver abated.

I was present at the Operation.

1675 Jan 6 I wore the Chain of Gold sent me from the King of Denmark, before the King in his Proceeding to the Chappel to offer Gold Frankincense and Myrrh.

20 The Earl of Winchelsea, Sir William Swan, and Mr Thinn were entertained at my Chamber in the Temple.

2ᵒ. This Afternoon I obtained the Earl Marshal's Leave to resign my Heralds Place.

Feb 10. Collonel Gervase Hollis, a Master of the Requests dyed.

21. Two Hor post Merid. I Sealed the Counterpart of Mr Hopkins, Mortgage of Little Pipe in Com. Stafford to me for 400 Pound.

25. Mr. Dethick offered me 300 Pounds, if I would resign my Heralds Place to him.

March 1 This Night Mr Sandford offered me the like Sum, if I would resign it to him.

9. Collonel Gervase Hollis's Body (was) carried thro London towards Mansfield in Nottinghamshire, where he was buried.

24 Lord Hatton and his Sisters Dined with me.

25 Mr Smith of Moorefields, dyed, he had an Excellent good Library of Books.

April 7 My Brother Dugdale having agreed with me for my Herald's Place this Morning moved

moved the Earl Marſhal that he might ſuc-
ceed me, which he granted.

The ſame Morning I agreed with my Car-
penter for building the additional Rooms I
made to my Houſe at *South-Lambeth*.

27 This Afternoon Sir *William Swan* told
me, the Prince Elector of *Brandenburgh* had
given Order for a Preſent to me, and that it
lay ready for me at *Hamburgh*.

May 1. Ten *Hor.* 30 Minutes *ante merid* I
and my Wife came to my Houſe at *South-Lambeth*, to lie there.

5. Ten *Hor.* 20 Minutes *ante merid* I laid
the firſt Stone of my New Building there.

20. This Day *Monſieur Swerene*, the Prince
Elector of *Brandenburgh's* Envoy came to Viſit
me at my Chamber in the *Temple*

25. My Wife in getting up of her Horſe
near *Farnham Caſtle*, fell down, and hurt the
hinder part of her Hand, and Left Shoulder.

June 6. Mr *Richard Hodgkinſon* (my old Friend,
and Fellow Gentleman of the Ordinance in
the Garriſon of *Oxford*) was buried.

25. Six *Hor.* 30 Minutes *ante merid.* the
Foundation of St. *Paul's* Church in *London*,
was laid

27 Dr. *Barlow* (my old and worthy Friend)
was Conſecrated Biſhop of *Lincoln*

July 15. This Morning a Iury of Sewers ſet out my Brick Wall made towards the
High-way, at my Houſe at *South-Lambeth*

21 Four *Hor. poſt merid.* I ſurrendered my
Heralds Place to his Majeſty in *Chancery*, be-

fore

fore Sir ——— Clerk, one of the Masters of that Court.

Aug. 28. One *Hor.* 40 Minutes *post merid.* I and my Wife came to dwell at my House in *South-Lambeth.*

Octob. 7. *Mons. la Mere* (lately sent from the Prince of *Orange* to his Majesty) gave me a Visit at my Chamber in the *Temple.*

8. I first became acquainted with *Monsieur Spanheim,* the Prince Elector *Palatines* Envoy to his Majesty, 9 *Hor* 30 Minutes *ante merid.* He was the Prince Elector *Palatines* Plenipotentiary at *Cologne,* and there Sir *Joseph Williamson* delivered to him my Book of the *Garter,* to present to the said Prince.

26. My Brother *Dugdale* was Created *Windsor* Herald.

27. Mr. *Thomas Ross* (Tutor to the Duke of *Monmouth*) dyed.

29. Between Nine and Ten *Hor. post merid,* my Uncle *Ralph Ashmole* dyed.

Novemb. 2. I fell Ill of a Cold.

7. Great Pain in my farther Tooth, on the left side of my upper Jaw, which continued three or four Days.

16. Eleven *Hor. ante merid* I began to plant my Garden Walls with Fruit-Trees.

This Day *Robert Chaloner, Lancaster* Herald, dyed.

Decemb. 4. I first became acquainted with Mr. *Butler,* Chaplain to the Duke of *Ormond,* and an able Astrologian.

1676. *Feb.* 27. Sir *Thomas Chicheley*, and Sir *Jonas Moore* came to Dine with me.

March 10. I fell Ill of the Tooth Ach, and the farthest Tooth in the upper side of my left Jaw, was very loose.

29. My Teeth fell looser, and put me to so great trouble, I could not chew my Meat for a Week.

31. My Brother *Harrison* of *Litchfield*, dyed.

April 6 I was afflicted with the *Vertigo*, and drew out my Tooth that had so greatly troubled me.

7 The Officers of Arms seeming unwilling to let me have the Funeral-turn, which was my due; I acquainted the Earl Marshal with it, and this Day, Sir *Thomas St. George* waiting on him, he told him, he would have me have the Benefit of it His Lordship afterwards told me, that he said to Sir *Thomas*, ' That he Esteemed me the best Officer in the Office, ' and if he could have perswaded me to have ' staid in the Office, I should not have wanted ' the best Employment, and have been made ' the Fore-Horse in the Team; and that I ' had deserved greatly, in getting Money for ' Re-building the Office.

Apr. 16. This Evening the Gout took me in my left Foot, and held me for a Fortnight

Aug 8 I fell ill of a Looseness, and had above Twenty Stools.

Septemb. 4 Mr. *Ogilby* dyed.

November 20 I fell ill of the Gout in my left Toe This Fit held me a Fortnight.

Decemb.

Decemb. 18. My old Friend Major *Brooke*, the Stationer. died.

22. He was buried.

1677. *Feb* 6. My Uncle *Ralph Afhmole's* Widow died

7 In the Afternoon I took cold in my Head.

14. I took cold in my right Ear.

19. Mr. *Richard Edlin*, one of my Clerks, died this Night.

20. Sir *Edward Walker*, *Garter*, died fuddenly

21, 23, 25. I took *Pile Macri* which did me much good.

21. Mr. *Richard Edlin* was buried in St *Alballows* Church-Yard

22 The Bifhop of *Salisbury* wrote to me, that he had moved the King to beftow *Garters* Place upon me I wrote back to excufe my accepting of it, with Defires to move no further on my Behalf

26. The Earl Marfhal fent his Secretary Mr *Hayes*, to have my Opinion, whether Garter's Place was in the Kings or his Difpofe. I gave my Opinion, that it was in the King's Difpofal

Mar 6 The Bifhop of *Salisbury* came to my Houfe. to acquaint me with the King's Command, that I fhould affift him in making good the Kings Title to *Garters* Place.

28. 7 *Hor ante merid* I laid the Foundation of my back Buildings to my Houfe at *South Lambeth.*

30 There was a Hearing before some of the Lords of the Council and some Knights of the Garter, between the King and Earl-Marshal, at which Garters Place was adjudged to be solely in the King's Disposal.

3.. Mr *Bartie* earnestly pressed me to accept of *Garters* Place, intimating my Lord Treasurer thought me fittest for it, which I excused, nevertheless he gave me an Opportunity to speak with my Lord, which when I had, I forebore saying any Thing of this Matter to him

Apr. 1 Mr. *Bartie* set more earnestly upon me to be *Garter*, but I absolutely refused.

2 My Father *Dugdale* was pitched upon to be *Garter*, and the King gave his Consent, whereupon the Earl Marshal sent for him out of *Warwickshire* by this Night's Post.

10. My Father *Dugdale* came to Town.

11 The Earl Marshal told my Father *Dugdale*, that I had carried my self very fairly in the matter between him and the King, touching *Carters* Place.

May 10. 9 *Hor. ante merid.* The first Foundation of the Rebuilding of *Cheapside* was laid.

12. About Noon I sprained my right Foot, near my Ancle

24. My Father *Dugdale* was created *Garter*, principal King at Arms.

25 He was Knighted.

June 1. He took his Oath in a Chapter, called to that Purpose.

7 My

7. My Lord Treasurer agreed to have my Comptrol continue upon the Vouchers.

July 2. I sealed a Lease of my House in *Litchfield* to Mr. *Falkingham* for Eight Years.

Another to *Henry Aldrich* of the Lands in *Homerich*. for Seven Years.

Another to Mr. *William Webb*, of the *Mogg*. in *Litchfield*, for Eleven Years.

10 I made a Feast at my House in *South-Lambeth*, in Honour of my Benefactors to my Work of the *Garter*

Aug. 1 I received 400 *l*. being the Mortgage Money I formerly lent upon Mr. *Hopkin's* Estate, at *little Pipe* near *Litchfie'd*

Sept 10 1 *Hor post merid.* Mr *Rose*, the King's Gardiner, died.

17. Count *Wallestein*. Envoy Extraordinary from the Emperor, Marquiss *de Este Borgamainers*, Envoy extraordinary from the King of *Spain*, Monsieur *Swerene*, Envoy Extraordinary from the Prince Elector of *Brandenburgh*, and the Count of *Flamburgh* bestowed a Visit on me at my House at *South-Lambeth*.

28. There was a Fire in the *Inner Temple*.

Oct 4. Mr *Loggan* began to draw my Picture in Black Lead

16 My Lord Bishop of *Oxford* gave me a Visit at Mr *Loggans*

31 *Myne Heere van Zeelin* (Secretary to the Prince of *Orange*) came to visit me at my Chamber in the *Temple*

Nov 4 Mr *Rawlins*, Town-Clerk of *Litchfield*, acquainted me, that Mr. *Richard Dyott*, Parliament-Man for that City, was likely to die,

die, and that the Bailiffs, &c. were willing to chuse me in his Room ; but I answered, I had no Inclination to accept of that Honour, and therefore desired him to give my Thanks to all that were so well affected to me.

10. *Myne Heere van Zeelin*, and the *Dutch* Embassadors came to my House to visit me.

Dec. 10. Doctor *Plot* (a) came to me, to request me to nominate him to be Reader at *Oxford*, of the Philosophical Lecture upon Natural things. I told him if the University liked him, he should have my Suffrage.

19. 2 *Hor. post merid.* Mrs. *Ogilby* died.

This Morning my Tooth, next my Foretooth, in my upper Jaw, was very loose, and I easily pulled it out.

Having received several Letters from *Litchfield*, to request me to stand for a Parliament-Man there , I at length consented, provided it was not too late , and upon attempting it by others for me, found it was so , for I found the Magistrates and Friends not so cordial to me as I expected, and therefore drew off and would not stand.

1678. *Feb.* 9. One of my middle Teeth, in my lower Jaw, was broke out while I was at Dinner

Mar. 23. The Gout took me in my right Toe.

Apr. 4 11 *Hor* 30 Minutes *ante merid*, my Wife told me, that Mrs. *Tredescant* was found drowned in her Pond. She was drowned the Day before about Noon, as appeared by some Circumstance

6 B

(a) See Appendix.

6. 8 *Hor. post merid.* She was buried in a Vault in *Lambeth* Church-Yard, where her Husband and his Son *John* had been formerly laid.

22. I removed the Pictures from Mrs. *Tredescant's* House to mine

May 11. My Lord Bishop of *Oxford* and Dr. *Nicholas*, Vice-Chancellor of *Oxford*, gave me a Visit at my House, 7 *Hor* 30 *Min. ante merid*

June 18. Mr. *Lea* and his Wife's Release to me of the 100 *l.* I was to pay after Mrs. *Tredescant's* Death, bears Date.

July 17. About 8 of the Clock this Morning I was served with a *Subpœna*, out of the *Chancery*, at Mr *Searles* Suit.

Aug. 5. The Earl of *Peterborough* came to visit me at my Chamber in the *Temple*, and to see my Collection of Coins.

Sept 28. I took my purging Pills.

29. I bled with *Leeches.*

1679. *Jan.* 26. 10 *Hor. post merid.* The Fire in the *Temple* began next Room to my Chamber, and burned my Library, &c.

Mar. 25. I entred upon the House and Ground adjoining to my House at *South Lambeth*, which Mr. *Bartholmew* let me a Lease of.

31. 9 *Hor.* 45 Minutes *ante merid.* Mr. *Bartholmew* sealed my Lease.

April I first became acquainted with the Lord *Roberts*

June 8. I went to Sir —— *Napier*, at *Great Linford* in *Buckinghamshire*, and came thither next Day 8 *Hor. post merid.*

14. I returned to *London.*

27 I visited Monsieur *Spanheim.*

Aug. 15. My Lord Grace of *Canterbury,* (Dr. *Sancroft*) came to visit me at my House, and spent a great Part of the Day with me in my Study.

25. Sir *Jonas Moore,* Surveyor of the Ordinance, and my old Friend, died.

Sept. 2 Sir *Jonas Moore* was buried in the *Tower-Church.*

About the End of *October* I was much troubled with the *Vertigo.*

1680. *Mar.* 15. 8 *post merid.* I fell ill of the Gout in my left great Toe.

20. It fell into my right great Toe, and this Fit held me for Five Weeks.

Apr. 17. My Wife fell ill of a Rheumatism.

June 28. The Countess of *Clarendon* came to visit me and my Wife.

July 28. The Archbishop of *Canterbury's* Sister and Niece came to visit my Wife.

Sept. 6. The Earl of *Radnor,* Lord President of the Council, with his Lady and Daughters, dined at my House.

15 5 *Hor.* 30 Minutes *post merid.* Sir *Charles Cotterell* presented me to the Prince Elector *Palatine,* in the Council-Chamber, whose Hand I kissed, and had much Discourse with him about the *Order of the Garter,* into which he was ready to be elected.

16. 2 *Hor. post merid.* I presented the said Prince with one of my Books of the *Garter;*

G   which

which he courteously received, and now I had much more Discourse with him.

18. Sir *Charles Cotterell* told me this Morning, that one of the Prince Elector's Gentlemen came to him the Day before, to desire me to dine with him this Day. Hereupon I attended him accordingly, and he placed me next himself, on his left Hand, and received me with great Respect, and when he rose, took me aside, and told me he had heard much of my Worth and Esteem, and desired to have a Correspondence with me, after he returned into his Country.

Sept 24 This Day between 11 and 12, my esteemed good Friend Mr. *John Stanesby* of *Clements-Inn* died. He fell sick at *Northampton* the 17*th* instant between 11 and 12 of the Clock, as he was coming towards *London*, from his native Country, *Derbyshire*. He was buried the 26*th* of *September* at Night, in a Vault, in St *Clement Danes* Church, under the Seats belonging to the Gentlemen of *Clements-Inn*. He gave me this Legacy by his Will, *viz. ITEM, I give to my honoured Friend* Elias Ashmole, *Esq, and his Wife, each of them a Ring of Twenty Shillings value, and likewise what Books in my Study he shall please to make Choice of (many of them being his noble Gift to me after I had lost many of my own by the Fire at my Chamber)*

The Prince Elector *Palatine*, at his Departure, on *September* 18. put a Medal of Gold into Sir *Charles Cotterell*'s Hands, which had his Father's Picture on the one side, and an Escotcheon of

his

his Arms on the other, fupported by a Lyon;
and bad him to deliver it to me, and to affure
me, that when he came home, he would alfo
fend me one of his own.

27. This Day, Sir *Charles Cotterell* fent me
the Medal

November 4. Mr *Bartholomew* fealed me a new
Leafe of my Houfe, &c. in *South Lambeth.*

16. I received from the Hands of Sir *Robert
Southwell,* lately return'd from *Berlin,* a gold
Chain with a Medal, from the Elector of *Brandenburgh* It is compofed of 90 Links of Phi-
lagreen Links in great Knobs, moft curious
Work. Upon the one Side is the Elector's
Effigie, on the other, the View of *Strallfund,*
and made upon the Rendition of that City
into his Hands. It weighs 22 Ounces.

20. I waited on the King, and acquainted
him with the Honour the Elector had done
me, and fhewed him tha Chain He liked it
well and commended the Workmanfhip

1681. *Feb.* 9 Mr *William Chiffinch* Clofet-
Keeper to the King, dined at my Houfe, and
then told me that his Nephew *Thomas Chiffinch*
(Son to *Thomas Chiffinch,* my moft worthy
Friend) died the Week before.

March 15 Between 9 and 1, m rid Mr.
butler the Minifter and Aftrologian brought me
acquainted with Sir *Edward Deering,* Brother to
Sir *Edward D ring* now one of the Lord Commiffioners of the Treafury.

Apr 5. Having been very lame in the Hollow
of my right Foot moft part of the Winter (occafioned,

cafioned as I fuppofe, by applying Poultefles to my Gout, which relaxed my Tendons) this Evening my Pains were fo entreafed I could fcarce go, and put me into fo great a Heat, that I became very feverifh, and my Urine pricked me fore as it came from me.

6. I took my ufual Sweat, which made me well, and ftrengthened my Tendons, fo that the next Day I went to *London*, and walked much up and down the Streets, without any Pain, at Night I became hot, and flept ill.

9. 11 *Hor*. 45. Minutes *poft merid*. I fell into a cold Fit of an Ague, which, with the hot Fit, held me feven Hours.

11. I took, early in the Morning, a good Dofe of *Elixir*, and hung Three Spiders about my Neck and they drove my Ague away. *Deo gratias*.

14 Dr. *Gunning*, Bifhop of *Ely*, came this Afternoon to vifit me at my Houfe, and ftaid in my Study till Night.

May 19 My worthy Friend and my Neighbour, both at the *Temple*, and in the Country, *Thomas Siderfin* Efq, died, near *Epfom*, about 4 *Hor. poft merid*.

24 Mr. *Siderfin* was buried in *Lambeth* Church.

25 At the End of Dinner Mr. *Lillys* left Side of his Mouth was drawn afide, but recovered again.

30 This Evening the dead Palfey feized on the left Side of my old Friend Mr. *William Lilly*, Aftrologer.

June

June 2. Mr. *Lilly* took a Vomit, at Night he took his Bed.

4. I went to visit him, but found him beyond Hope.

9. 3 *Hor. ante merid.* Mr *Lilly* died.

10. 8 *Hor. post merid* He was buried in the Chancel of *Walton* Church

12. I bought Mr. *Lilly's* Library of Books of his Widow for 50 *l*

12 I sold one of my Chambers at the *Temple* to Mr. —————— *Holt*, for 138 *l* and in this Evening he was admitted.

17 This Day my God-Daughter —————— the only Child of my Neighbour *Thomas Siderfin*, Esq, died.

July 1 Mr *Sawbridge* the Stationer, an old Friend of Mr. *Lilly's* and mine, died.

6 Mr *Sawbridge* was buried in the middle Ile of St. *Bridget* Church in *Fleet-street.*

This Day my Wife went towards *Blyth-Hall*, with Sir *William Dugdale*, her Father, to visit her Mother.

Aug. 12. Sir *George Wharton* died at *Enfield* between One and Two in the Morning

18 My Wife returned from *Blyth-Hall*

25. Sir *George Wharton* was buried in the *Tower.*

Sept 19 My Wife miscarried, having gone about 3 Months

October 1 I took purging Physick.

2 I took my Sweat for Prevention of the Gout.

G 3   4. About

4. About 8 *Hor. ante merid.* I fell sick of the Cholick, which held me with sharp Pains, especially on my right Side for 24 *Hor* and then I was presently eased, by applying Bay-Salt and Bran, heated in a Frying-Pan, but before nothing else could ease me.

24. Mr. *Thomas Flatman* came to my House to visit me.

Nov. 1. Mrs. *Lilly* came to my House, and stayed a Week.

4. About 9 *Hor. ante merid.* I sealed an Assignment of my Judgment of 1200 *l.* formerly given me by Sir *Robert Thomas*, and about an Hour after, received from Sir *Robert Clayton* 800 *l.* a Composition, agreed on with Sir *Robert Thomas*, out of which I gave him 70 *l.*

Dec. 18. (*a*) About 4 *post merid.* my dear Mother-in-Law, the Lady *Dugdale*, died.

21. She was buried in a Sepulcher made in the Chancel of *Shuftock* Church, by Sir *William Dugdale*. for himself and her.

1682. *Mar* 10. About 5 *Hor. post merid.* I received a Summons, to appear at a Lodge to be held the next Day at *Masons Hall* in *London*.

11. Accordingly I went, and about Noon were admitted into the Fellowship of Free-Masons, by Sir *William Wilson*, Knight; Captain *Richard Borthwick* Mr. *William Wodman*, Mr. *William Grey*, Mr. *Samuel Taylour*, and Mr. *William Wise*

I was the *Senior* Fellow among them (it be-

(*a*) Vide *last* Page of Sir W Dugdale's Life —
Lond. 1714. 8°. ing

ing 35 Years since I was admitted) there was present besides my self the Fellows after named, Mr. *Thomas Wise*, Master of the *Masons-Company* this present Year ; Mr. *Thomas Shorthose*, Mr. *Thomas Shadbolt*, —— *Waidsfford*, Esq, Mr. *Nicholas Young*, Mr. *John Shorthose*, Mr. *William Hamon*, Mr. *John Thompson*, and Mr. *William Santon*. We all dined at the *Half-Moon-Tavern* in *Cheapside*, at a noble Dinner prepared at the Charge of the new accepted *Masons*.

Apr. 1. My Wife fell ill of a Rheumatism ; it began in her left Ancle, then into her left Knee and right Toe.

18. Sir *Charles Cotterell* carried me to the *Morocco* Embassador.

Alçade, *Abdelloe*, and *Bomonzore* came to my House, and dined with me.

May 17. *George Smaldridge* was elected out of *Westminster-School* to go to *Christ-Church* in *Oxford*.

20. The Marquis of *Worcester* and Earl of *Aylesbury*, with their eldest Sons, gave me a Visit at my House this Afternoon.

22 This Night, scratching the right Side of my Buttocks, above the Fundament, thence proceeded a violent sharp Humour.

25. I applied Poultesses thereunto (and now was not able to sit or lie upon my Bed) it was made of white Bread-Crums, Oil of Roses and Rose-Leaves.

28. The Poultesses having well drawn the Humour out, I applied *Unguentum Nutritium* to it.

June 4. Being hard bound in my Body I was Five Hours before I could go to Stool, and suffered much Torment.

9. I

9. I purged with Pills.

13. I went abroad again, Thanks be to God.

17. *Bomonzore* dined with me, and gave me several excellent Receipts.

July 5. The *Morocco* Embassadour dined at my House.

13. The Astrologer's Feast was restored by Mr. *Moxon*.

16. The Lord *Lansdown*, and Sir *William Haward* gave me a kind Visit at my House.

20. The *Moroceo* Embassadour made ready to go away, but the *Alcade* slipt out of his Lodgings, and hindered his Journey.

21. The *Alcade* was taken.

22. This Morning I gave the *Morocco* Embassadour a large magnifying Glass. In the Afternoon the *Alcade* returned to the Embassadour's Lodgings.

23 About 3 in the Morning the Embassadour went away

Aug 16. I went towards *Oxford*, to see the Building prepared to receive my Rarities, where I arrived about 7 of the Clock in the Evening.

17. Between 8 and 9, I first saw the said Building I was invited by the Vice-Chancellor, and dined with him at *Queen's-College*.

22 6 Hor. 30 Minutes *post merid* I arrived back at my House

Oct. 23 My Lord Chancellour *Finch* sent for me to cure him of his Rheumatism. I dined there, but would not undertake the Cure

1683. *Jan.* 23. I took a great Cold, going by Water, and kept my Chamber Three Days.

29 The Astrologers Feast was held at the Three *Cranes* in *Chancery-Lane*, Sir *Edward Deering* and the Town-Clerk of *London* were Stewards.

Feb. 2 My Picture (after sent to *Oxford*) came home 3 *Hor. post merid.* I acquainted Mr. *Woolrich* in part, with the Secret of raising Flowers from a Virgin-Earth.

15. I began to put up my Rarities in Cases to send to *Oxford*.

Mar. 7. I took purging Pills, which wrought very well.

10 The Gout fell into my left great Toe this Morning

14. The last Load of my Rarities were sent to the Barge, and this Afternoon I relapsed into the Gout.

21 The Gout fell into my right great Toe.

Apr. 8. Major *Huntington* came to my House, to visit me.

10. I took my Pills, and purged very well.

11. The Pains in my Feet returned.

24 Mr. *Antbony Bowyer*, and his Lady came to visit me and my Wife.

25 I went first abroad after so long Confinement, by Reason of my Gout.

26 Dr. *Smallwood*, Dean of *Litchfield*, died.

Aug. 6 The Surveyors of the High-Ways began to raise the Causey at *Horshead-Still*.

9 They finished their Work, all at my Charge

Sep. 5. I took Pills.

6. I

6. I took a Sweat.

7. I took Leeches, all wrought very well.

17. Monsieur *Job Ludolph* came to visit me.

23. I first saw Dr. *Lister*, at my Lord Archbishop of *Canterbury's* at Dinner

24 The Prince Elector of the *Rhine's* Secretary dined with me. As also a Nobleman of that Country, a Son of a Patrician of *Nurembergh*, and Dr. *Lister*.

26. A Stitch took me at the setting on of my left Hip.

28, I was very much troubled with it.

Oct 8 Monsieur *Ludolph*, and his Son, dined with me.

10 I gave Mr *Hyseg* a Book of the *Garter*, my Wife gave him Three gold Buckles.

16. The Commissioners of the Excise dined with me

30 I took leave of Monsieur *Ludolph*, and his Son who were returning into *Germany*.

Nov Monsieur *Ludolph* went from *London*.

Dec. 7. A Boil began under my Chin

26. 6 *Hor.* 30 Minutes *ante merid.* I had a long Fit of a Vertigo

1684 *Feb* 4 Mr *Jean Schielderas*, the Bishop of *Bergn's* Son and Mr *Godfreed Ross*, a *Prussian*, visited me

Mar. 5. 11 *Hor. ante merd* a green Staff was sent me by the Steward of St *Thomas's* Hospital with a Signification that I was chosen one of the Governours.

Apr 6 Major *Huntingdon* dined with me.

8 There was an Installation of *George*, Prince of *Denmark*

21. Major *Huntingdon* died, and this Day Mr. *Thomas Henſhaw*, Dr. *Rogers*, Dr. *More*, and Dr. *Bernard* dined at my Houſe.

30. Major *Huntingdon* was buried at St. *Botolph Alderſgate* Church.

May 5. 2 *Hor. poſt merid.* I laid the Foundation of my new Stable.

14. I took a Sweat.

19. Sir *Thomas Walcot* came to viſit me.

June 27. I bruiſed my left great Toe

July 18. 10 *Hor.* 18 Minutes *ante merid.* my two Coach-Horſes were brought to me.

22. My Coach was brought to me.

23. I went towards *Oxford*.

28. I returned Home.

Aug. 4. Several *French* Gentlemen, and *Johannes Serenius Chodowieskey*, a *Polander*, came to viſit me

6 I rubbed the Skin near my Rump, whereupon it began to be very ſore.

8 I purged.

9 I took *Leeches*.

10 I purged again.

12 I applied a Plaiſter to it.

15 Mr. *Agur* applied a Balſam.

17 The Sore began to break

18 Dr. *Plott*, ſent from *Oxford* to viſit me, came to me

19 I fell into a Looſeneſs, which continued for Two Days

24. Mr. *Agur* launched the Sore

26 Being hard bound, I was Two Hours before I could go to Stool, and then with exceeding great Trouble.

3I. I

31. I was launched again, to prevent a Fistula.

Sept. 10. By this Time; the Sore, near my Fundament, was healed.

Oct. 20. Sir *Thomas Duped*, and Mr. *Matthews* dined with me.

Nov. 19. Dr. *Plott* presented me with his Book *de Origine Fontium*, which he had dedicated to me.

24. My Teeth began to be loose.

Dec. 8. Mr. *Haak* brought Mr. *Bowen* of *Upton* in *Pembrokeshire*, to visit me.

19. Dr. *Chamberlain* proposed to me to bring Dr. *Lister* to my Wife, that he might undertake her.

22. They both came to my House, and Dr. *Lister* did undertake her.

1685 *Jan.* 24. I was much troubled with my Teeth, in my upper Jaw, on my left Side, which, by Fits, continued for a Week, and then I held Pills in my Mouth, made of burned Allom, Pepper, and Tobacco, which drew much Rheum from me, and so I was eased.

Feb. 6. King *Charles* II. my gracious Master, died.

14 About 9 *post merid.* he was buried.

13. I took a violent Cold, which held me till the 5th of next Month.

26. I took my purging Pills.

27 I took my Sweat, both worked very well.

March 2. 5 *Hor.* 15, Minutes *post merid.* I received an obliging Letter from the Bailiffs, Justices

stices, &c. of *Litchfield*; so also from the Dean, inviting me to stand to be one of their Burgesses for Parliament. I sent them Word that I would stand.

3. Whereupon they set about getting Votes for me, and I found the Citizens very affectionate and hearty. About a Fortnight after my Lord *Dartmouth* told me, the King would take it kindly from me, if I would give way to Mr. *Lewson*. Upon this I applied my self to my Lord Treasurer, and desired to know of him the King's Pleasure, by whom I found it was the King's Desire, and then I immediately wrote down, to acquaint my Friends that I would resign; but they would not believe my Letter, which occasioned me to go to the King, and let him know so much, who told me he did not know I stood, when he gave Mr. *Lewson* Encouragement to go down, for if he had, he would not have done it, I told him I was all Obedience, which he took very kindly. I then wrote down again, to assure them I would sit down, and so Mr. *Lewson*, with the Assistance of my Votes, carried it at the Day of Election.

Apr. 11 *8 Hor. post merid.* I first became acquainted with Mr. *Negos*, Secretary to the Duke of *Norfolk*.

27. Mr. ―― of *Nuremberg*, and a *French* Gentleman, which Mr. *Labadie* brought along with him, dined with me.

May 1. Judge *Walcot*, and Mr. *Cook*, the Prothonotary dined with me.

H   4. Mon-

4. Monsieur *Spanheim*, Envoy extraordinary from the Elector of *Brandenburgh*, and his Lady, and Monsieur *Bessor*, his Agent here, with Sir *Charles Cotterell*, his Lady, and Son, dined with me.

5. The Duke of *Norfolk* invited me to dine with him the next Day, which I did, and was well received.

13 I took my purging Pills.

14. And my Sweat.

29. I visited Dr. *Smith*, Bishop of *Carlisle*, who was of my ancient Acquaintance at *Oxford*.

31. This Night again a Pain (in my Sleep) took me in my middle Toe of my right Foot, which removed to my Ancle, and after Three Days went away.

June 2. A Pain took the uppermost Tooth but one, on the right Side of my uppermost Jaw.

4. My said Tooth sunk so low I could not chew.

9 A Boil rose in the left Side of my Throat.

17 This Evening I had a grievous Fit of the Tooth-Ach.

July 9. The Countess of *Clarendon*, Bishop of St *Asaph*, Mr. *Henshaw*, Mr. *Evelyn*, Dr. *Tenison*, and Mr. *Frasier* supped at my House.

11. The Earl of *Radnor* fell sick about Noon.

17 1 *Hor. post merid.* The Earl of *Radnor* died.

20. Dr. *Ridgley* (my old Acquaintance) gave me a Visit.

21. I went to *Windsor*, to the Installation of the Duke of *Norfolk*, Earl of *Peterborough*, and Lord Treasurer

25 The Earl of *Radnor's* Body was carried into *Cornwall*

Aug 4 I and my Wife went to Mr *Noruus* at *Brockhill*.

5 We went to Mr. *Hutchinsons* at *Dchut*

6 We returned Home

10. A Boil began to appear in my right Groin

13 This Night my Boil broke

15 Another appeared a little higher, but it died

24 I went to *Windsor*, to the Installation of the Earl of *Feversham*

Sept 5 Passing upon the *Thames*, I took a great Cold.

9 I took a Purge

10 I took a Sweat

Oct 13 I took my Sweat.

28 The Earl of *Peterborough* shewed me his rare Collection of Gemms and antient Rings

30 I became acquainted with Mr. *Cary*, who came lately from *Berlin*, he told me his Electoral Highness of *Brandenburgh* did often speak, with a great deal of Honour, of me and designed to have my Book of the *Garter* translated into *Dutch*

Nov 10 This Morning I had some Discourse with Mr *Gerard*, about purchasing Mr. *Plommers* Farm.

16 Mr Dean of *Windfor*, and Dr *Chamberlain* the Civilian, brought Sir *John Faulconer* of *Scotland.* to dine with me, I found him a very ingenious Gentleman well read in his own Country Antiquities and Coins.

Dec 3 I first sat upon the Commiffioners of Sewers it being opened this Morning, and my felf named therein, but nothing further was done at this fitting

14 Sir *John Faulconer* dined with me, and I gave him divers of my *Englifh* Coins

16 I waited on the Earl of *Clarendon*, Lord Lieutenant of *Ireland*, as far as *St. Albans* in his Journey thither The jolting of the Coach, which drove very hard, raifed a Swelling in my l.f. Breech

1686 *Jan.* 9. Mr. *Cook*, my Neighbour at *South-Lambeth*, having lately fet up a pale along his Garden. and encroached upon the Church-Way about Two Foot, I undertook to complain of it and this Day Mr *Cooper*, his Land-lord, and my felf upon a Debate on the Matter agreed (by his Confent) to fet it back a Foot and an Half which was done accordingly

20 The Commiffioners of Sewers met, and I (with fome others of the Commiffioners) took my Oath

Feb 1 Sir *John Faulconer*, a *Scotch* Gentleman died.

4. He was buried this Night in the Church of St *Margaret Weftminfter*

10. This Morning I dreamed. that being at my old Houfe in *Sheere-Lane,* the Side of the Gar-

Garrat seemed to totter and fall, insomuch that I thought the House it self would presently fall down.

This Afternoon, about One of the Clock, my Wife's Father, Sir *William Dugdale*, died.

14 I moved the Duke of *Norfolk*, on my Brother *Dugdale*'s Behalf, that he would move the King, that he might succeed him, which he promised to do, (but I found him more inclinable to prefer Sir *Thomas St. George*) In his Discourse he told me, no Man was fitter for the Place than my self, if I would accept of it, but I made the same Excuse to him, as I did to his Father, after the Death of Sir *Edward* *ker*

19 The Duke of *Norfolk* proposed to me to give my Brother *Dugdale* the Place of *Norry*, and the next Day gave him Assurance of it.

March 26 This Night I pist so much that I feared a Diabetes, notwithstanding I had kept my self very temperate all the Spring-me.

27 This Morning I grew ill and very hot, and was troubled with a Sharpness of Urine I took Syrrup of White Lillies in Posset-drink and the next Day an Emulsion of the four co ... Seeds (this kept me temperate) with W .... Violets and Wood-Bine, to wash my Mout , and giving my self Rest and Ease, I thank .... I recovered in a few Days

5 I took my Sweat

My Wife took Dr. *Nagel*'s Tincture

17. I first dined at St. *Thomas's* Hospital, the general Court being held there this Day.

20 11 *Hor* 15 Minutes *ante merid* I first sat upon the Commission for Charitable Uses.

23 Dr *Plot* presented me with his Natural History of *Staffordshire*

26 Mr *Plummer* sealed his Part of the Conveyance of the Farm to me, and his Wife acknowledged a Fine before the Chief Justice of the *Common Pleas*

July 1 This Morning early the Fang-Tooth in the right Side of my upper Jaw fell out

13 I began to repair my Barn at *South-Lambeth* for Goodman *Ingram*

25 I took my Sweat

Aug. 2 I and my Wife went to *Brockhill* to Mr *Norton*

— We went to *Dooe* to Mr *Hutchinsons*

5 We returned to *South-Lambeth*

— The Gout fell into my left great Toe I applied Leeches

25 I applied black Snails to my right Foot that being bruised, but they blistered and poisoned the Top of my Foot, and after several Breakings out it was healed towards the middle of *October*

Sept. 8 I took my usual Sweat.

25 5 *Hor.* 10 Minutes *post merid* I agreed upon Conditions with Goodman *Ingram* to take a Lease of the Farm I bought of Mr *Plummer*, except the Oat Field

— Sir *Philip Floyd* (who had the Reversion of my Office in the Excise) died

Oct. 7. I waited upon the King, upon his Return to Town from *Windsor*, who was pleased to receive me with much Kindness.

12. I took a great Cold in my Neck, which held me Six Days.

25 6 *Hor* 45 *post merid.* I sealed the Lease to *John Ingram.*

26. The running Gout seized on my Wife's right Instop. It continued shifting into her Arms and Knees with great Torment till after *Easter*, and then she began to set her Feet on the Ground, yet was not able to go abroad till towards *Midsummer*

2y I received a Letter from Sir *Henry Chaun-* ry, Treasurer of the *Temple,* to invite me to the Bench, but I wrote him an Excuse, and next Day gave him Reasons for my Refusal.

Dec. The Commissioners of Excise moved the Lord Treasurer, shewing the Necessity of my having another Clerk, and obtain'd Set per ann Salary for him.

23 10 *Hor* 30 Minutes *the mer* I received my Order from the Lord Treasurer, for a new Clerk, with 80 *l. per Ann* Salary

23 This Day my Nephew *Dug* (Sir *J hn Dugdale*'s Son) was married

1687 *Jan* 5 The Earl of *Rochester* surrendered his Staff

About 6 *post mer* the Commission for the Lord Commissioners was opened and read

5 This Morning the Commissioners of Excise and my self waited on the new Lords Commissioners of the Treasury.

13. The Gout fell into my right Hand, which difabled me from ufing my Pen for above a Quarter of a Year.

16. I took my Sweat

17, 18, 19 I was much troubled with the Wind-Cholick.

24. I applied Leeches to my right Hand

27 The Swelling of my Hand abated.

28 There were two Tides this Morning.

Feb 8 This Afternoon the Gout fwelled my Hand again and the Night paffed with great Torment

4. This Night my Hand did moft grievoufly pain me

March 3. This Afternoon I and my Wife were both fuddenly ftruck with a Cold and Hoarfenefs

I felt the Effects of this Hoarfenefs in the back Part of my Throat for a long Time after

22 2 Hours Minutes *poft merid.* An Iffue was made in my left Arm

Apr 16 My Wife took Mr *Bigg's* Vomit which wrought very well

19. She took *Tutus Sanctus* in the Afternoon, fhe took cold

N S That both were too ftrong Phyfick for her

2 My Wife fell very ill and into a great Weaknefs

25 I purged with my ufual Pills

27 I took my ufual Sweat

Towards the End of this Month my Wife began to mend but not fully recover till a Fortnight after

July 16 This Morning I received a Parcel of Books from *J W. Irnhoff* of *Nurembergh*, among which was his *Excellentium Familiarum in Gallia Genealogia*

Aug 31. Sir *John Chardin*, and Mr. *Bever*, came to *South-Lambeth* to visit me.

Sept. 14 12 Hor. 40 Minutes *ante merid.* I set for a second Picture to Mr *Ryley*

Oct 5 11 Hor. 7 Minutes *ante merid* the Earl Marshal's-Court first sat in the Painted-Chamber at *Westminster*

— Dr. *Plot* came to me at my Office and told me that the Earl Marshal had chosen him Register of the Court

8 10 Hor. *ante merid.* I went first to the Earl Marshal's Court, and when his Lordship rose, he invited me to dine with him which I did

9. I took my usual Sweat. (*a*)

W HAT remains further, I shall give you in the Words of Mr. *John Aubrey*, F R. S. who in his designed *Survey of the County of Surry*, (reposited in the *Ashmolean Museum* at *Oxford*) towards the Beginning has these Words —— ' And now I am come as a " a Mourner to perform my last Office at the ' Grave of my worthy Friend *Elias Ashmole*, Esq, ' whose Body lieth buried in the *South* Ile (of ' the Church of *South-Lambeth*) at the East End, on the *North* Side of it, under a black Marble with this Inscription.

H.

(*a*) Here ends Mr. Ashmole's M. S.

Hic jacet Inclytus Ille & Eruditiſſimus

ELIAS ASHMOLE Leichfeldenſis Armiger,

inter alia in Republica Munera,

Tribut. n Cervifias Contra Rotulator,

Fœd s autem Windſorienſis *titulo*

per annos plurimos dignatus,

Qui poſt duo connubia in Uxorem duxit tertiam

Elizabetham GULIELMI DUGDALE

Militis, Garteri, Principalis Regis Armorum filiam,

Mortem ob t 1º Mai, 1692 anno ætatis 76

Sed durante Muſeo ASHMOLEANO, Oxon.

nunquam moriturus

Near it, is an Atchievement ſet up for the ſame Perſon, wher on is the following Coat of Arms viz Quarterly Sable and Or, the firſt Quarter on a Fleur de lis, of the ſecond impaling Dugdal, viz Argent a Croſs moline Gules and a Torteaux with this Motto ---

Ex ara omnis ———

Over the Entrance to the Muſeum, fronting the Street, the following Inſcription in Capital Letters

Muſeum Aſhmol anum, Scentia Naturalis Hiſtoriæ Officina Chymica

Over the Door of Mr. *Afhmole's* Library, at
the Top of the Stairs, is the following Infcription, in Letters of Gold, *viz.*

Libri Impreffi & Manufcripti e donis Clariff. Vi-
rorum D. Eliæ Afhmole & Martini Lifter Qui-
bus non paucos addidit Vir induftrias nec infime de
Re Antiquariâ Promeritus D. Johannes Aubrey de
Lafton Peirce apud Wiltonienfes Arm. & Soc.
Reg. Sociæ.

AN

APPENDIX

Of Original Letters fent to, and from Mr. Afhmole.

A Letter of Thanks from the Corporation of Litchfeld, upon the Receipt of a Silver Bowl, Prefented to them by Mr. Afhmole.

For the truly Honoured *Elias Afhmole*, Efq, at his Chamber in the *Middle Temple*, over Serjeant *Maynard's* Chamber. In his Abfence to be left with the Batler or Porter of the *Middle-Temple London.*

Honour'd Sir

UPon Thurfday, being the 17th Day of this Inftant *January* (a Day ever to be *Rubric'd* amongft our City Remembrances) we received your *Tina Argentea*, your munificent Silver Bowl, cloathed

cloathed in its Delivery, with all those Rich
Circumſtances of Advantage, that could poſſibly either enable the Gift to beſpeak the Good-
neſs and Prudence of the Giver, or invite the
faireſt Acceptation in the Receiver For if we
conſider the Perſon from whom It is the Gift
of an *Elias*, a Herald, not only Proclaiming,
but actually Contributing good Things to our
City, and that by the Hands of a *Zacharias*, a
faithful Meſſenger, who with the Gift, did em-
phatically communicate the Serie and good Affection of the Giver And if we conſider the
time it was Preſented, It was the Day of our
Epiphany Seſſions of the Peace for the City,
where our Bailiffs High-Steward, Sheriff,
Grand Jury, and the reſt of the Body Politick
of this Antient and Loyal Corporation together with other Perſons of Quality, both of
the Clergy and Laity were convened together,
and ſo became preſent at this great Offering
As if ſome propitious Stars ariſing in the Eaſt,
had (at this time) gone before our *Magis*, Steer-
ing its Courſe to this our City of *Lichfield* (the
Sarepta of our *Elias*) and ſtood over the New-
Erected Pyramids of our Cathedral (where is
yet a Star appears) darting its benign Influence
upon this Poor and Loyal City inviting the
Magi from afar, to offer ſome Tribute to it:
A City that hath nothing to glory in, but its
Antient and Modern Loyalty to God and
Ceſar, evidenced by her antient *Bearing* in the
City Eſcotcheon (three Knights martyred) as
antient as the Days of *Dioclſian*, and her

I   Name

Name fignifying a Field of Blood then fpilt, to
which may be well added her Modern and un-
parallelled Loyalty to that Bleſſed Saint (now
in Heaven) King *Charles* the Martyr, Univer-
ſaly witneſſed by thoſe honourable Marks,
Braces, and Wounds of Loyalty, ſhe yet bears
upon her Perſons Temples Streets and Walls,
(Trophies of Honour) ſufficiently blazing to the
World the true Heraldry of her ancient Arms,
nor have you only given us this great *Cratera*
upon which you have wifely impreſt our City-
Arms) to ſhall the duſt of the City after their
Time of Suffering but like one of thoſe true
Xns, that offered to Chriſt in his pooreſt Conditions you have largely offered to the Repair
of in Church our ruined Cathedral, which,
by the in earned Labour Prudence Piety and
Charge of our good ſir, Biſhop a ſecond *Ceada*,
ſ the Charity of your ſelf, and others hap-
ly poſted in his Hands, almost to a Mi-
racle and to you reſtored again. But
you have liberally offer-
ed relieved and refreſhed Chriſt in his Mem-
bers the Poor of our City. And as if you intended you to ingroſs and cover all our Ne-
ceſſe under that warm and nouriſhing Man-
receiving Intimation of your
Good intended this great
Leave to conclude that
by informing you
Deſire, upon the firſt
Re-

Receipt of your *Poculum Charitatis* at the Sign
of the *George* for *England*) we filled it with Ca-
tholick Wine, and devoted it a sober Health to
our most gracious King, which (being of so
large a Continent, past the Hands of Thirty to
pledge, nor did we forget you. 't in the next
Place, being our great M.......diting you
that (God willing) we shall the Court, this
this great T. i Argente shall with our City
Mace, and other publick Insigns of Dignity and
Authority, be carefully transmitted, by Inden-
ture, from Bailiffs to Bailiffs, in a continual
Succession, so long as this ardent and loyal
Corporation through the Favour of Princes
(which we hope, we shall never forfeit) shall
have a Charter to give it Life and Being. For
which End your many other multiplied Favours
to this poor City We the present Bailiffs of this
City do, in the Name (and by the Defire) of
our whole Company return you most hearty
Thanks, subscribing our selves what we truly
are,

   S I R,

        Your obliged faithful Friends,

Litchfeld 26.   T......
Jan. 1656.

            John Barnes,
            Hen. Baker.

A Preface to the Catalogue of Archbishop Laud's Medals, drawn up by Mr. Ashmole, and preserved in the publick Library at Oxford, and referred to in Page 41 of this Work.

CUM Oxonium (bene audit lumen orbis ... grandeque decus, commen-
... gratia ... aliquot ante me contulissem,
Collegio Regalis Præpositi (tunc temporis autem in incluta hac Universitate, Proto Bibliothe-
carii Bodleian.) Doctoris Barlow postulatio, imo
& expostulatio me non mediocriter afficere.

Querebatur enim eximiæ doctrinæ Vir, inter
Academicos (temporibus difficillimis illis quidem & tyrannide Cromwelliana invalescente, du-
rissimis paucos tum superesset plurimis artis &
naturæ dotibus suspiciendis, Ostracismo etiam-
num pulsis aut (nec vanus timor) propediem
pellerdi, qui ad rei Antiquariæ studium &
veterum Numismatum cognitionem, quibus tamen affatim illic abundent Archiva (paupertate
& nova tyrannide pressi, adjecissent animum.
Supra laudati Doctoris inquam rogatu conque-
stuque, hoc ultro mihimet ut brevem illorum
descriptionem exhiberem) pensum imposui
Tum ad novitios & in rei Nummariæ scientia

parum

parum exercitatos, melius informandos, tum ad
eorum Genium excitandum, qui ad tantum, tam
proficuum, tam dignum, tam honorificum, tam
denique necessarium erudito viro studium aspi-
rare niterentur

Hoc igitur sic mihi propositum sponteque
susceptum (arduum illud quidem, & laboriosæ
plenum opus aleæ pensum) latus aggredior, indies
factione *Cromwelliana*, non sine damno publico
ingravescente, & paulo post Britanniæ παλιγ-
γενεσίαν & sacræ Regiæ Majestatis (auspicato
& quasi postliminio) reditum, σὺν θεῷ ad
finem perduxi Sed cum hujus exscriptum, ma-
nu propria cuperem exarare, ut ingenue fatear,
mihi fuit ἀδύνατον ante hunc diem illud ab
solvere, cum negotiorum (quæ me continuo
circumvallat) turba, modicum mihi subinde
spatium, ad aliquid per intervalla & quasi fur-
tim nonnunquam ex eo transcribendum pro-
miserit Verum antequam huic Operi conti-
nando te Lector accingas de nonnullis, & ad
promptiorem ejus diligentiam, & ad faciliorem
quidem usum te monitum cupio

Atque ut aggrediar, totum opus de antiqua
Numismati quibus ora diteicunt Archiva,
in tria dividitur Volumina Primum est Consu-
larium Nummorum aliquosque *Illustrium Roma-*
norum reliqua duo *Imperatoria Numismata* continent

Huc accedit, quod Monetam Consulum A
phabetico locarim ordine potius quam illam
in annorum Consulatus cujusque seriem redi-
gam Multi etiam Consulares Nummi nequa-

I ᴣ

quam ab iis, quibus affimilantur, excufi funt.
Sed ab illis Triumviris Monetalibus *Augufti* reg-
no, qui vellent ifta ratione vel quod forfan ab
ipfis ducerent originem, ut præclaras illorum
actiones aliquot exciperet, actueretur æternitas.
Quod autem attinet ad *Imperiales* Nummos (qui
hic incipiunt a *Julio Cæfare*, atque cum *Herac*
definunt, hi ad eos perfecte referuntur annos, in
quibus conflati, procufque fuere, cum relatio-
ne tamen ad tempus vel præcedens, vel fubfe-
quens Incarnationem *Chrifti* Salvatoris* noftri,
quod characteribus iftis expreffi, A C. hoc eft,
ante Incarnationem *Chrifti*, & J C id eft, ab
Incarnatione *Chrifti*. Qui characteres notantur in
capite cujuflibet paginæ, paucis exceptis, qui
fufficiens ad hoc ut ad manifeftam fui temporis
cognitionem deducere me queart, lumen defde-
rare videntur. Atque ifto quidem fub *Impe*-
ratoris cujufque regni finem, Anno ante eofdem
in margine nullo defignato, collocar cnam eofdem cætero inter intrudere certa five ratione
faci eligi. Iacum ac ita *Imperiales* omnes
eadem eju os rationem a me præftitum ef

Præterea, ut ex quo genere metalli, quolibet
bet ex eis Numifmatis cui no eft conftare
poit, metall per nas fequentes diftinxi notas
AV erum denotat ira, AR indicat
dei qu nz t t Æ

orro cum Ænei Num ni diverfæ magnitudi-
exiftan ad triplicem præfertim (quæ d
nantur, juxta numericas figuras ( ) (&
characteribus norum præfixas (exceptis
ib ar r atis aliquot qui pecul

ariter pro talibus exhibentur) ad triplicem, inquam, præcipue magnitudinem, revocari poffunt.

Adde fuperioribus, quod ubi quempiam argenteum Nummum, formam habentem fecundæ magnitudinis æreorum invenio, quod ut duxtaxat ab ordinario diftinguatur Denario, figuram illi (2) foleam adjungere.

Hanc, hoc gemino cum voto, præfatiunculam claudere mihi eft animus, D O M enixe deprecatus, tum ut generoforum hâc in parte Benefactorum numerum adaugeat Tum ut eos qui prifca Numifmata celeberrimum hoc in Ærarium conferunt, novis, quibus fuam fublevent inopiam, Numifmatis, nunquam egere, patiatur.

Pene omiferam quemlibet poft annum, hic a me de induftria relictum effe fpatium, ut quid è novo dictum ad Thefaurum, antiqui ferentur Nummi, ad hunc quoque Catalogum, pari (quo fuperiores) modo, referri valeant

Scriptum in meo Me-
dio Templi Mu-
fæ, decimo Ca-
lendas Junias,
Anno Jul. 1666

E. Ashmole.

A Copy

A Copy of a Letter from Doctor Barlow to Mr. Ashmole, on his Present of his Books, describing Archbishop Laud's Cabinet of Medals.

For my Honoured Friend *Elias Ashmole*, Esq, at his Chamber in the *Middle Temple*, these; *London*.

My dear Friend,

IT is a good while since I received your excellent Present to our University-Library, and 'ere this told you so, and returned our many and hearty Thanks had I not been suddenly and unexpectedly call'd away to *Here After* whence I am now returned At the Visitation of *Bodlys Library* (when the Vice Chancellor and all the Curators were met) I presented your Book to the Vice-Chancellor and the rest in your Name a a Testimony of your Kindness and Love to Learning and our University, as also of your Ability to enrich *Bodlys Library* with your own Works Any Man who has a Mind to read your Works, may give us good Books of other Men making but

y y

very few of their own, *pauci quos æquus amavit Jupiter* Some more generous and ingenuous Souls, a *Selder*, a *Dugdale*, or an *Ashmole* may do this none else. The Vice-Chancellor and the Curators were exceeding well satisfied with and very thankful for your great Charity and Munificence to the Publick Care is taken, that your Name and Gift be recorded in our Register (a) to your deserved Honour, and the Incouragement of others, by your good Example, if not to an Equal yet to a like Liberality And sure I am it will be an Honour to you and a Comfort to your friends when they shall find in our Register, that you have been so great a Benefactor to Bodley's Library My Love and Respects to your self and my honest Friend Mr *Dugdale*, God Almighty bless you both, And,

    S I R,

           Your affectionate Friend,

Queen's College, Ox-
   on *Decemb.* 28.
  1668

        Thomas Barlow.

               For

For *Elias Ashmole*, Esq; at his House in *Lambeth*.

SIR

THE Bearer hereof will need no Recommendation from me when you shall understand that it is Doctor ___, the Learned Author of the natural History of Oxfordshire. It is upon the Reputation of your own Worth as well as your magnificent Cities intended to the University that he ___ the Art ___ to be better known to you. They are (I hear) designing to ___ a Philosophical Lecture upon Natural Things and their Inclination to pitch upon this following Gentleman for that Purpose whose Talent and Merits are so eminent I am Sure cannot miss of your concurrent Suffrage I am ___ sorry that the Affair which carries him this Morning out of Town deprives me of so desirable an Opportunity of kissing your Hand at *Lambeth* who am for many great Obligations,

SIR

Your most ___

___ Servant

W___ ___

D___ ___

J. EVELYN

For

For the Worshipful and Learned *Elias Ashmole*, Esq, at his House in *South-Lambeth*, near *London*.

Most worthy and learned Sir,

BEING informed by my Friend Mr *Gadbury*, that there were several Passages in my History, which did some way reflect on your great Worth and Learning, and also intimate me to be guilty of gross Rudeness and Heat. I found it my Duty to make this Recantation, and so let you know that whatever in that Kind may occurr, I utterly repent and disown, and am both heartily sorry and ashamed that any way I should prove so unhappy, offensive to so good and learned, so industrious and renowned a Gentleman whose Books I am not worthy to bear after him. And Sir, if it will please you to let me see a Copy of the Passages, as you have collected them, (which on Occasion I promise to return, with your Confutations and Remarks) I do solemnly protest that I will make a publick Recantation, or other ways as you shall think fit, and also if ever King Henry's or this another Impression I will alter those Passages as far as Truth and Equity shall require; still protesting in Truth and duty, that I never had any but Honourable

ble and respectful Thoughts of you and Sir
William Dugdale, (*Dii! quanta nomina*) and what
I did, proceeded from a Desire of finding out
the Truth, however my Frailty might betray
me to an Error, Sir, the Honour of a Line,
especially with an Intimation of your good
Will, will be highly acceptable to the real
Honourer of your Learning and Goodness.

Emanuel College, **Camb.**
  Oct. 15. 1688.

Joshua Barnes.

   My humble Duty to his Grace at *Lambeth*,
and pray Sir, have me recommended to my
good Master Doctor Gale and Mr *Gadbury*,
&c.

For my worthy Friend Mr *Joshua
Barnes*, at *Emanuel-College* in *Cam-
bridge*

   S I R,

MY present weak Indisposition has took
me off from too much resenting those
Reflections you have made on me in your
Book

Book, * and moulded in me more peaceable Thoughts, than to be disturbed at what you have done. Your Letter makes me think there was no ill Meaning in what you did, and perhaps nothing more than an Inadvertent and overhasty Humour, which the Civility of a Penny-Post Letter would have cleared and prevented. I need not trouble my self, nor you with giving you an Account of those Passages that concern me, they are easily found out, for they carry my Name along with them. All I expect from you is, that your Acknowledgments to others (as you have Occasion) be what you have now made to me, and (if ever an Opportunity be offered) to reprint your History, then to rectifie your Copy,

SIR,

I am,

Your Humble Servant,

Octob.
16 5.

E. Ashmole.

K r

---

* The History of King Edward the IIId. &c. wherein Mr. Barnes reflected on Mr. Ashmole's Order of the Garter, in a wrong &c. Mr. ...

A Copy of a Letter from the Chapter of the Church of Litchfeld to Mr. Ashmole, communicated from the Registers of that Cathedral.

Honoured Sir,

Whatever Interest this City and Church have in your Birth and Education, hath already redounded, in so much Honour thereby, and in your continual Bounty, to both That we have not the Confidence to back with that Topick, our Petition for our free Gift towards finishing the Ring of Ten Bells, instead of our former Six bad and useless ones Nor in Truth have we any other Arguments, but your Charity and our Necessity, of the former, you have given us Proof as we acknowledge with all Thankfulness And of the latter, we have too much, through the Misfortunes of the first The Decayedness of the Ground first making our first Bell-Founder lose his casting the biggest to the Damage of 30 *l.* and now his Error in oversizing the Eight, he hath cast so far that they have swalowed up all the Metal for the Ten, and that

re-

requires 80 *l.* more to be added to our poor
Fund for the two other Bells, proportionable
to that Bigneſs. But yet an Error ſo much
on the better Hand, that would make extream-
ly for the Advantage and Glory of the Cathedral (the Bigneſs of ſuch a Ring far more
befitting the Place, and theſe Eight being
judged ſo very good, that all are loth to have
them broken, and caſt into leſs) if poſſibly
that additional Sum could be raiſed. To this
Purpoſe Eſq; *Dmt*, Mr. *Walmiſley*, the Sub-
Chantor, and other Vicars, and Ringers are
moſt induſtriouſly undertaking a new Collection, and We and ſeveral others are willing
a-new to contribute, and if you will pleaſe to
put to the helping Hand of your Piety and
Muniſicence, you will add ſignally to thoſe In-
ſtances thereof already in our publick Catalogue of Benefactors, and will highly oblige
both thoſe zealous Undertakers, and eſpecially,

S I R,

your thankful humble Servants

Litchfeld,
Oct. 16.
889

LANC. ADDISON,
HEN GRESWOLD,
THO BROWNE,
JO HUTCHINSON,
CHRIS COMYN.

F I N I S.

Lightning Source UK Ltd.
Milton Keynes UK
UKOW05f2042260318
320073UK00008B/86/P

9 781170 563007